Mission

We understand "community literacy" as the domain for literacy work that exists outside of mainstream educational and work institutions. It can be found in programs devoted to adult education, early childhood education, reading initiatives, lifelong learning, workplace literacy, or work with marginalized populations, but it can also be found in more informal, *ad hoc* projects.

For us, literacy is defined as the realm where attention is paid not just to content or to knowledge but to the symbolic means by which it is represented and used. Thus, literacy makes reference not just to letters and to text but to other multimodal and technological representations as well. We publish work that contributes to the field's emerging methodologies and research agendas.

Subscriptions

We are pleased to offer subscriptions to *CLJ*—two issues per year:

Institutions & libraries	$200.00
Faculty	$30.00
Graduate students & community workers	$20.00

Please send a check or money order made out to the University of Arizona Foundation to:

John Warnock, *Community Literacy Journal*
445 Modern Languages Bldg., University of Arizona, P.O. Box 210067
Tucson, AZ 85721
Info: johnw@u.arizona.edu

Cover Art

Cover art for this issue of *Community Literacy Journal* was designed by Guest Editor Adela C. Licona around the issue's theme of Youth, Sexuality, Health, and Rights.

Editorial Advisory Board

Jonathan Alexander	*University of California, Irvine*
Nancy Guerra Barron	*Northern Arizona University*
David Barton	*Lancaster University, UK*
David Blakesley	*Clemson University*
Melody Bowdon	*University of Central Florida*
Tara Brabazon	*University of Brighton, UK*
Danika Brown	*University of Texas–Pan American*
Ernesto Cardenal	*Casa de los Tres Mundos, Managua*
Marilyn Cooper	*Michigan Technological University*
Linda Flower	*Carnegie Mellon University*
Diana George	*Virginia Tech University*
Jeff Grabill	*Michigan State University*
Greg Hart	*Tucson Area Literacy Coalition*
Shirley Brice Heath	*Stanford University*
Tobi Jacobi	*Colorado State University*
Lou Johnson	*River Parishes YMCA, New Orleans*
Paula Mathieu	*Boston College*
Regina Mokgokong	*Project Literacy, Pretoria, South Africa*
Ruth E. Ray	*Wayne State University*
Georgia Rhoades	*Appalachian State University*
Mike Rose	*University of California, Los Angeles*
Tiffany Rousculp	*Salt Lake Community College*
Cynthia Selfe	*The Ohio State University*
Tanya Shuy	*National Institute for Literacy*
Vanderlei de Souza	*Faculdade de Tecnologia de Indaiatuba, São Paulo*
John Trimbur	*Worcester Polytechnic Institute*
Christopher Wilkey	*Northern Kentucky University*

COMMUNITY LITERACY *journal*

Editors	Michael R. Moore DePaul University
	John Warnock University of Arizona
Senior Assistant Editor	Amanda Gaddam DePaul University
Journal Manager	Daniel James Carroll DePaul University
Design & Production Editor	Kimberly Coon DePaul University
Book & New Media Review Editor	Jim Bowman St. John Fisher College
Social Media Editor	Melissa Pompos University of Central Florida
Consulting Editors	Eric Plattner DePaul University
	Stephanie Vie Fort Lewis College
	Rachael Wendler Univerity of Arizona

Submissions

The peer-reviewed *Community Literacy Journal* seeks contributions for upcoming issues. We welcome submissions that address social, cultural, rhetorical, or institutional aspects of community literacy; we particularly welcome pieces authored in collaboration with community partners.

Manuscripts should be submitted according to the standards of the *MLA Handbook for Writers of Research Papers*, 7th ed. (New York: MLA).

Shorter and longer pieces are acceptable (8–25 manuscript pages) depending on authors' approaches. Case studies, reflective pieces, scholarly articles, etc., are all welcome.

To submit manuscripts, visit our site—communityliteracy.org—and register as an author. Send queries to Michael Moore: mmoore46@depaul.edu.

Advertising

The Community Literacy Journal welcomes advertising. The journal is published twice annually, in the Fall and Spring (Nov. and Mar.). Deadlines for advertising are two months prior to publication (Sept. and Jan.).

Ad Sizes and Pricing

Half page (trim size 6X4.5)	$200
Full page (trim size 6X9)	$350
Inside back cover (trim size 6X9)	$500
Inside front cover (trim size 6X9)	$600

Format

We accept .PDF, .JPG, .TIF or .EPS. All advertising images should be camera-ready and have a resolution of 300 dpi. For more information, please contact Michael Moore: mmoore46@depaul.edu.

Copyright © 2013 Community Literacy Journal
ISSN 1555-9734

Community Literacy Journal is a member of the Council of Editors of Learned Journals

Printing and distribution managed by Parlor Press.

fall 2013

Volume 8 Issue 1 Fall 2013

Special Issue: Youth, Sexuality, Health, and Rights
Guest Edited by Adela C. Licona and Stephen T. Russell

Table of Contents

Articles

Transdisciplinary and Community Literacies: Shifting Discourses and Practices through New Paradigms of Public Scholarship and Action-Oriented Research 1
Adela C. Licona and Stephen T. Russell

Education/Connection/Action: Community Literacies and Shared Knowledges as Creative Productions for Social Justice 9
Adela C. Licona and J. Sarah Gonzales

Empower Latino Youth (ELAYO): Leveraging Youth Voice to Inform the Public Debate on Pregnancy, Parenting and Education 21
Elodia Villaseñor, Miguel Alcalá, Ena Suseth Valladares, Miguel A. Torres, Vanessa Mercado, and Cynthia A. Gómez

Addressing Economic Devastation and Built Environment Degradation to Prevent Violence: A Photovoice Project of Detroit Youth Passages 41
Louis F. Graham, Armando Matiz Reyes, William Lopez, Alana Gracey, Rachel C. Snow, and Mark B. Padilla

Paying to Listen: Notes from a Survey of Sexual Commerce 53
Rachel C. Snow, Angela Williams, Curtis Collins, Jessica Moorman, Tomas Rangel, Audrey Barick, Crystal Clay, Armando Matiz Reyes

Moving Past Assumptions: Recognizing Parents as Allies in Promoting the Sexual Literacies of Adolescents through a University-Community Collaboration... 71
Stacey S. Horn, Christina R. Peter, Timothy B. Tasker, and Shannon Sullivan

Poetry

Public Speaking 91
Niki Herd

Man 93
Zack Taylor

Boom 96
Sammy Dominguez and Zach Taylor

Zine

Project Connect Zine 99

Book and New Media Reviews

Slam School: Learning Through Conflict in the Hip-Hop and Spoken Word Classroom 117
Reviewed by Amanda Fields

Valuing Youth Voices and Differences through Community Literacy Projects: Review of Detroit Future Youth Curriculum Mixtape and *Freeing Ourselves: A Guide to Health and Self-Love for Brown Bois* 121
Reviewed by Londie T. Martin

Respect Yourself, Protect Yourself: Latina Girls and Sexual Identity 127
Reviewed by Lorena Garcia

Transdisciplinary and Community Literacies: Shifting Discourses and Practices through New Paradigms of Public Scholarship and Action-Oriented Research

Adela C. Licona and Stephen T. Russell

In 2010, we received a nationally competitive grant from the Ford Foundation to undertake cross-disciplinary, community-engaged work to shift public conversations around youth sexuality, health, and rights (YSHR). We came to the projects from our positions as a humanities scholar (Licona) and as a social science scholar (Russell). According to the Ford Foundation, "a deeper understanding of human sexuality is an essential element of human rights and healthy social relationships." Beginning with this assumption, we seek to be informed by and to inform policies and local practices; to initiate broad conversations that address sexual health and healthy sexualities for youth; and ultimately to develop innovative collaborations, programs, and research.

We proposed and were funded to: 1) engage in action-oriented research; 2) train cross-disciplinary sexuality scholars; and 3) produce strategic communications that would allow for our collaborative research to circulate meaningfully throughout academic and non-academic contexts. Community literacies are relevant to each of these goals, as they must necessarily inform participatory research and its circulation. By "community literacies" we mean not only the lived, relational, and situated knowledges that circulate in and across communities, but also the ways in which those knowledges are produced and communicated.

With our funding, we established the Crossroads Collaborative, a *think-and-do tank* that brings together University of Arizona faculty, postdoctoral research associates, graduate student scholars, youth-oriented community partners, and local youth to understand what and how young people learn about the dimensions and intersections of the full spectrum of their identities and what it all means for their sexualities, health, rights, and well-being. Our grant was one of six such grants in the US that year. Instead of taking already established research agendas to a community, grantees worked to develop their research agendas *with* communities to address topics deemed by the community to be locally relevant and connected to youth sexuality, health, and rights (YSHR). The projects that were funded, and are delineated in this special issue, hold the potential to critically and creatively address the possibilities and constraints that often exist simultaneously in community contexts. These local possibilities and constraints aid and/or prohibit youth access to sexuality and health knowledge, information, and resources that are basic human rights. The same possibilities and constraints are at play when youth attempt to express themselves about these issues and others regarding their sexual and gender identities. Articles here highlight the ways in which literacy practices produce and inform, as well as are produced and informed by, these very possibilities and constraints and the broad social issues, relations, policies, and practices from which they emerge.

Our own research at the Crossroads Collaborative began in a context of "legislated intolerance,"[1] which initiated and enforced restrictions on particular bodies, groups of people, and bodies of knowledge. After Arizona became known as having passed the most regressive anti-immigrant and anti-immigration legislation in decades, other states quickly followed suit. Through our collaborations at this historic moment, we worked with youth who responded to repressive conditions with creativity, knowledge, curiosity, and advocacy. In yearly grantee gatherings, we learned that others shared similar experiences with youth in their communities. Across projects, we learned that youth care: they are interested in learning, and in participating in learning environments that are respectful, meaningful, and culturally relevant. They have dreams, desires, ideas, and demands, as well as fears and uncertainties. They are interested in productive social change, particularly regarding issues that affect their lives as multiply situated historic and sexual subjects. Across these diverse research/community collaborations, we learned that changing the status quo requires increased understanding of youth perspectives and support for amplifying their voices, and their multi-modal literacies, as they claim their collective right to knowledges that are meaningful to their lives. The projects in this special collection demonstrate multiple approaches to understanding youth perspectives, including approaches that are implicitly and explicitly about the literacies that informed and contextualized each project. Such situated literacies[2] were expressed and exchanged between community organizations and academic institutions, youth and community researchers in youth-serving organizations, and action-oriented academic researchers.

For this special issue, we sought submissions that feature innovative "research with respect"[3] and the possibility for reciprocity; that address theoretical, methodological, pedagogical, and/or policy implications; that attend to how research is undertaken by academic and non-academic community members, and is translated and made legible across community contexts for the explicit purpose of social change; that include and highlight youth voice and vision; and/or that creatively bring stories and numbers together in participatory action-oriented research.[4] We circulated our call to other Ford Foundation grantees and explained our approach as one that considers each of us, and our community collaborators, "literacy workers." We defined "literacy work" as work that is relational, informed by community concerns, considers community members as knowledgeable, treats community histories as meaningful, makes people and places knowable and understandable to one another across contexts, and is oriented toward social change.

By making such innovative, cross-disciplinary practices visible and legible here, we hope to inspire other change-oriented research collaborations. In keeping with this journal's priorities, we are pleased that community and academic researchers have co-authored every article. Such collaborations effectively move beyond the division that can exist between the academy and the community and the knowledges that circulate and are produced therein. We have included individual and collaborative work by youth in our local communities; by emerging sexuality scholars; and by poets whose work inspired us and offered meaningful insight into lived experiences, dreams, desires, disappointments, and righteous anger. Each article manifests an approach to literacy that insists on valuing knowledges that emerge from the inside-out and the bottom-up. More importantly, each article works to use these literacies to make communities intelligible as historical agents of knowledge production. Resulting shifts to the limiting and often pathologizing discourses of youth sexualities, health, and rights can be used to inform best practices.

In "Education/Connection/Action: Community Literacies and Shared Knowledges as Creative Productions for Social Justice," Adela C. Licona and J. Sarah Gonzales share details of their community/academic collaborations in the context of a summer camp in which youth participants, together with adult allies, were treated as knowledgeable, capable, and interested in both the acquisition and production of knowledges. Such an approach allowed participants to be treated as teacher/researchers—each with something to teach, and something to learn. Through the community pedagogy of ECA, and with an emphasis on relational literacy and participatory media, youth rendered their individual and community histories, as well as other topics of perceived urgency, understandable to one another. Participants together explored the possibilities for connection across contexts that might facilitate coalitional action during a time of particularly egregious and politicized restrictions on the knowledge, information, and resources available to youth.

In "Empower Latino Youth (ELAYO): Leveraging Youth Voice to Inform the Public Debate on Pregnancy, Parenting and Education," academic and community collaborators write about and demonstrate the *how-tos* of engagement in participatory action research with and for youth. Their article contributes to the teacher/researcher literacies that have emerged in this special issue within projects that teach the foundations of community-based research to young people across multiple levels of formal and informal education. With this foundation, young people become active in policy-relevant and practice-based research designed to intervene in deficit-driven discourses as well as to highlight issues critical to Latino youths' sexual and reproductive health and educational rights.

In "Addressing Economic Devastation and Built Environment Degradation to Prevent Violence: A Photovoice Project of Detroit Youth Passages," youth and adult authors offer a glimpse of what youth see in their everyday spaces, how they see it, and, even more importantly, how they are re-visioning and re-creating it. Members of the Youth Advisory Board of Detroit Youth Passages, with the assistance of project researchers, learned to use photography as a tool for discovery and storytelling. In their article, they analyze their own photographic representations to effect two important interventions. First, through their photographs and accompanying narratives, a different Detroit—one that is lived in and loved—is introduced and made visible. Secondly, their visions effect a youth-informed structural critique that insists that viewers understand themselves as implicated in Detroit's economic and environmental devastation, explicitly linking these conditions to violence. Youth make themselves known as persons invested in the vibrancy of their city spaces. Lived knowledges that re-contextualize and re-historicize Detroit emerge in this photo essay as community literacies that can and should inform policy efforts, particularly concerning youth communities.

In "Paying to Listen: Notes from a Survey of Sexual Commerce," colleagues from the Detroit Youth Passages team engage in self-reflection to interrogate the practice of "paying to listen." The authors offer an elucidating discussion of the challenges and potentials of listening to and learning from young people involved in sexual commerce. As one reviewer for this manuscript noted, this work "touches on methodological issues often left unexamined in sexuality research, community-based and participatory research, and ethnographic studies." Through the intimacies revealed in their shared field notes, the authors confront distinct goals and protocols for researchers and literacy workers situated in community-based organizations and those situated in the research university. They question what research with marginalized youth can accomplish, grapple with the ethical challenges of their research, and conclude that reflection, progressive learning, and ethical listening must be a part of participatory research that is committed to social change and social justice with and for youth.

In "Moving Past Assumptions: Repositioning Parents as Allies in Promoting the Sexual Literacies of Adolescents through a University-Community Collaboration," the collaborators in Project Safe SPACES (Social Pressures, Attitudes, Culture and Experiences related to Sexuality) call us to understand parents through an asset-based framework in research and advocacy concerning sexual education and sexual/ity literacies. Parents are often considered only as obstacles to progressive and comprehensive sexual education; the research team recognized that this presumption deserved interrogation. In the team's research, parents emerged as potential allies in the effort to secure young people's access to sexual knowledges and develop their sexual literacies. From this perspective, parents can be understood as community literacy workers who are distinctively positioned to facilitate sexual literacies for young people that can promote healthy sexualities and healthy relationships.

Our special issue would be incomplete without consideration of the rhetorical force and function of poetic voice. Slam poetry, as noted in Adela's and Sarah's report, has emerged in Tucson as a coalitional practice of civic engagement for a number of different youth groups, and serves as a critical and creative tool for discovery, protest, and historic narration—it is, fundamentally, an expression of youth-driven civic engagements and community literacies. For this reason, we invited submissions from youth slam poets involved in the Tucson Youth Poetry Slam. "Man," by Zack Taylor, intervenes in normative assumptions and expectations about what it means to be a man. In this poem, Zack slams about the right to sexual and gender nonconformity, particularly around expressions of masculinity. In "Boom," slam poets Sammy Dominguez and Zack Taylor creatively and critically engage the realities of everyday bullying across contexts.[5] Through their collaborative slam poem, we are reminded of the many ways in which young people experience ordinary spaces as threatening, and how educational contexts can fail to be inclusive spaces of meaningful learning. These poets use statistics about LGBTQ suicide together with the names of young people who have died by suicide—numbers and stories—to call attention to the mundane nature of everyday harassment and everyday violences. Spitting on the mic, Sammy and Zack use this performance to illuminate the intolerances that can prevail in climates where sexual and cultural literacies are restricted by normative expectations.

We also invited a submission from Niki Herd, whose poetry is simultaneously real, raw, and hopeful. She is a storyteller whose voice lends a particular urgency to our discussion of youth, sexuality, health, and rights, with a focus on the gender and sexual dimensions of young lives. In "Public Speaking," Herd connects erased historical knowledges, invisibilities of gender non-conforming youth, and bullying, to reveal the everyday risks of expressing non-normative sexualities and genders. Her poetry returns us to legislated intolerance and the need for education to contest such misinformed and still powerful practices. Her lyrical and poignant prose also invites us to witness the hopeful image of a young person "model-walking freedom" and "expressing confidence in youth and a young sexuality."

We are particularly pleased to include *Project Connect: Youth Power,* a collaborative zine produced with contributions by youth activists from four of the Ford Foundation-funded research projects in Chicago, Detroit, San Francisco, and Tucson. Youth contributors got to know each other via a cross-country, multi-modal curriculum designed by J. Sarah Gonzales, who facilitated the participatory production of the zine through a series of video exchanges in which youth introduced themselves and their communities, initiated conversations around YSHR, and considered the possibilities for ongoing collaborations and alliances. Through their video dialogues and shared writings, youth served as (media) literacy workers who taught one another about their home communities as well as about local issues pertaining to YSHR, including teen Latina parenting and LGBTQ rights. They co-produced this zine to "show solidarity, inspire long-term activism, and build community." Their zine demonstrates that contributors understand themselves as part of a larger collective power and that the right to knowledge and resources around a broad understanding of sexualities is of crucial importance to youth across the country. Through this multimedia collaboration, they came to see more clearly that youth both alike and different from themselves are making change in their communities.

Our special issue ends with reviews written by Crossroads scholars Amanda Fields, Londie Martin, and Jenna Vinson highlighting texts relevant to scholars and activists who are informed by the goals and principles of action-oriented literacy scholarship. By engaging, (1) the history and meanings of slam poetry and hip-hop pedagogy in and beyond the (conflicted) classroom; (2) Latina lives and sexualities; (3) digital youth curricula that address contemporary sexualities; and (4) sexuality and health education for communities of diverse and fluid gender identities and expressions; these reviews collectively address the power and potential of storytelling, arts-based literacies, sexual and gender literacies, and multi-modal and place-based literacies to inform formal and informal curricula and research agendas committed to social justice.

Through our traditional and non-traditional approaches to community research and community literacies, we hope to have advanced an understanding of the promise and potential of reciprocal and relational literacies, highlighting how these can inform asset-driven approaches to youth knowledges, community knowlegs, action-oriented and policy-relevant research, cross-disciplinary graduate training, and public conversations about YSHR. Through each project, diverse teams of academics, community organizers, students, and youth engage in collective inquiries that offer innovative examples of meaningful engagement with diverse community literacies in the pursuit of social change in the areas of youth, sexuality, health, and rights.

Acknowledgments

We would like to thank the Ford Foundation for their vision and support. We are also grateful to our fellow Ford Foundation grantees across the US for their inspiring work and contributions to this special issue. We thank youth-serving community collaborators and participating youth across all projects. Finally, we offer thanks to the editors and editorial staff at the *Community Literacy Journal*, members of the Crossroads Collaborative, and to Ray Moody and Leah Stauber for their editorial assistance.

Endnotes

1. Prescott College's Chair of Humanities, Randall Amster, J.D., Ph.D., has referred to the legislation emerging from Arizona's 49th legislature as part of a larger drive toward legislated intolerance.

2. See David Barton, Mary Hamilton, and Roz Ivanič, <u>Situated Literacies: Theorising Reading and Writing in Context</u> (New York: Routledge, 2000), and Kate Pahl and Sally Kelly, "Family Literacy as a Third Space between Home and School: Some Case Studies of Practice," <u>Literacy</u>, 39 (2005): 91-96.

3. Our use of "research with respect" is inspired by the University of Arizona's Knowledge River program's 2010 panel discussion titled "Research with Respect: Ethical Approaches to Native American Cultural Research and Archival Practices," which addressed research integrity in action-oriented scholarly projects with non-dominant and indigenous communities.

4. For us, the act of making something, someone, or someplace legible or intelligible can be understood as both a literacy event (see Shirley Brice Heath, "What No Bedtime Story Means: Narrative Skills at Home and School," <u>Language in Society</u>, 11 (1982): 49–76) and a literacy practice.

5. Readers can access Sammy's and Zack's slam performance of "Boom" from the Brave New Voices 2012 Competition in Berkeley, CA on the Tucson Youth Poetry Slam YouTube channel. Go to Sammy D & Zack T (Team Tucson—Brave New Voices 2012). Their performance is also accessible through the Community Literacy Journal website.

Adela C. Licona, Ph.D., is co-director of the Crossroads Collaborative and associate professor in Rhetoric, Composition, and the Teaching of English at the University of Arizona. She is affiliated faculty in Gender and Women's Studies, the Institute for LGBT Studies, Family Studies and Human Development, and Mexican American Studies. Her interdisciplinary research and teaching interests include borderlands rhetorics, cultural and gender studies, social justice coalitions, and alternative media, as well as community literacies and action-oriented research. Adela is co-founder of Feminist Action Research in Rhetoric, FARR, a group of feminist scholars engaged in public scholarship and community dialogue. She is co-editor of *Feminist Pedagogy: Looking Back to Move Forward* (Johns Hopkins University Press, 2009) and author of *Zines In Third Space: Radical Cooperation and Borderlands Rhetoric* (SUNY Press, 2012). She can be reached at aclicona@email.arizona.edu.

Stephen T. Russell is co-director of the Crossroads Collaborative and Interim Director of the John and Doris Norton School of Family and Consumer Sciences at the University of Arizona. He is also Distinguished Professor and Fitch Nesbitt Endowed Chair in Family and Consumer Sciences, and Director of the Frances McClelland Institute for Children, Youth, and Families. Stephen conducts research on adolescent pregnancy and parenting, cultural influences on parent-adolescent relationships, and the health and development of lesbian, gay, bisexual, and transgender (LGBT) youth. He received a Wayne F. Placek Award from the American Psychological Foundation (2000), was a William T. Grant Foundation Scholar (2001-2006), a Distinguished Investigator of the American Foundation for Suicide Prevention (2009-2011), a board member of the National Council on Family Relations (2005-2008), and was elected as a member of the International Academy of Sex Research in 2004. He is President of the Society for Research on Adolescence. He can be reached at strussell@arizona.edu.

Education/Connection/Action: Community Literacies and Shared Knowledges as Creative Productions for Social Justice

Adela C. Licona and J. Sarah Gonzales

This article highlights Education/Connection/Action (ECA), a locally developed community pedagogy deployed at a youth activism summer camp that served as a site for a community/academic teaching and research collaboration. Youth considered connections between a set of issues, including a local ban on Ethnic Studies, the School-to-Prison Pipeline, and Youth Sexuality, Health, and Rights. They drew from lived and learned literacies to inform participatory media projects that critically and creatively address restrictions on access to local knowledges and information with particular relevance to youth sexuality, health, and rights (broadly defined). In highlighting youth voices, desires, and needs across distinct youth communities, their collaborative productions demonstrate coalitional potential and a collective call for change.

We, the youth, believe abstinence-only is not acceptable.
Comprehensive sex education is not promoting sex, but knowledge.
It's better to be aware, informed, and prepared instead of ignorant and fearful of change.
We are a new generation.
We are change, tolerance, and understanding.
No longer streets gathered of polychromatic lowriders and the competition of Macho Men stuck through cities and cries of "no homo."
We need purified love, acceptance, forgiveness, understanding, and bravery for change.
We, the youth, want love, no more ignorant love.

– Alexia Vazquez & Enrique Garcia, TYPS Poets & Nuestra Voz Racial Justice Summer Camp Participants, 2011

The poem above, titled "No More Ignorant Love," instantiates the powerful, and powerfully creative, work written and performed at the 3rd Annual Nuestra Voz: Youth, Art and Activism Summer Camp. It reflects the arts-based approach engaged throughout the camp, while also elucidating the potential of using art to discuss and act on civic and social justice issues. Alexia, a high school senior, and Enrique, a high school junior, co-wrote this poem at the end of a series of roundtables that introduced participants to youth-identified themes of interest including the Ethnic Studies Ban (Arizona state laws ARS §§ 15-111 and ARS §§ 15-112), the School-to-Prison Pipeline, and Youth, Sexuality, Health, and Rights. In these roundtables, youth used their own lived experiences, interests, and desires to inform the discussions, and collaborated on action projects. The poem is an expression of an emergent consciousness about the interlocking relationship between sex, gender, race, and class and, thus, it served a pedagogical purpose in the camp by positioning poets as peer educators.

In this report we intend to explore both the pedagogical strategies that enable young people, such as Alexia and Enrique, to emerge as poets and peer educators, and the collaborative approaches that support such strategies. We introduce a framework developed by community literacy practitioner J. Sarah Gonzales, the *Education / Connection / Action* (ECA) approach, and describe the ways that our collaboration around arts-based inquiry informed a number of youth-led productions. Youth were supported in their desire to speak back to the authoritative discourses pathologizing activist youth and to speak up regarding constraints on their pursuits of knowledge, interests, needs, and dreams. First, however, we will provide some background about the development of our particular collaboration, along with the contexts that framed the summer camp.

Creative Space for Youth under Fire: Background and Context

We (J. Sarah Gonzales and Adela C. Licona) came together initially around our shared interest in racial justice.[1] Gonzales served as Director of the Racial Justice Program, including the Nuestra Voz Latin@ Youth Initiative summer camp, at the YWCA Tucson. Licona is Co-Director of the Crossroads Collaborative at the University of Arizona, a project funded by the Ford Foundation to foster action-oriented research collaborations that seek to understand the constraints and possibilities around what youth know, what they want and need to know, and how they learn about sexuality, health, and rights. We both believe in the need for critical community education, and we each work on issues of social justice from our distinct locations in a community-serving organization and at a public university. We were interested in collaborating on issues of racial justice, sexual and gender justice, as well as immigrant/immigration, economic, and reproductive justice. We each positioned ourselves as adult allies to local youth, and to the youth movements that were emerging in Tucson as a response to regressive legislation in the state of Arizona.

We started our collaboration in the midst of a political climate that fueled, and was fueled by, social panic expressed in particularly regressive legislation with dramatic implications for youth participants (see Herdt, 2009, on moral and sexual panics). It was a time marked by the passage of such legislation as SB 1070, officially named the "Support Our Law Enforcement and Safe Neighborhoods Act" but popularly referred to as the anti-immigrant, anti-immigration, "papers please" legislation. This act was considered among the most restrictive pieces of anti-immigrant legislation in the U.S. when it initially passed through the Arizona state legislature in 2010. Many youth participants felt threatened by this legislation because of its sanctioning of racial profiling, and because either they or their family members held differing immigration statuses.

Arizona House Bill (HB) 2281 (which later became state laws ARS §§ 15-111 and ARS §§ 15-112), popularly known as the ban on Ethnic Studies, was also a part of the suite of panic-inflected legislation. This bill prohibits public and charter schools in Arizona from promoting either the "overthrow of the U.S. government" or "resentment toward a particular race or class of people" and from advocating ethnic solidarity or curriculum designed for a "particular ethnic group." It was passed to ban the teaching of Mexican American Studies in the Tucson Unified School District, the largest district in the city; the law threatened other Ethnic Studies programs in the state as well (Basu; Planas). Youth experienced the ban as a restriction on their right to learn from and access culturally relevant material in their classroom contexts. The legislation fueled a youth movement that itself also fed into the panic that defined the Arizona legislature at this time. Several camp participants were active in protesting the Ethnic Studies ban at the local and state levels.

Finally, a bill that received far less media attention, but was nonetheless a part of the panic-inflected legislation, was Senate Bill (SB) 1309, known as the Parent's Bill of Rights. This bill, like HB 2281, functioned to restrict students' access to knowledge and rights regarding their own health and sexual education by granting parents the right to opt students out of classes with any sexual content. The fervor in the local community was heightened by the intensity of national and global media in the city, and by the regularly occurring youth-organized protests.

In response to this local context, we planned a social justice summer camp focused on art as activist expression, using youth-created multimodal productions to move their voices into public spaces where decisions were being made. Licona joined the weekly planning meetings in anticipation of the camp, and participated as a volunteer and teacher-researcher at the weeklong summer camp directed by Gonzales. As community workers, activists, and researchers, we came to know, and opened ourselves to learn from, one another. Our roles in our collaborations became that of action-oriented teacher-researcher with one another as well as with the youth (see Licona and Russell, in preparation), as we sought to develop guiding principles and strategies for facilitating community education, connection, reflection, and action explicitly with and for youth participants (see Mitchell on action research and new social movement mobilization).

The *Education / Connection / Action* (ECA) Approach: Applied Principles of Community Literacy and Action-Oriented Collaborations

It was in the context of YWCA Tucson's Racial Justice Program that Gonzales actively developed and began to implement the Education/Connection/Action (ECA) approach, which aims to build pedagogical practices that honor spaces and practices of community education. ECA begins with a commitment to engaging local histories with an understanding of youth as knowledgeable and as interested in learning.[2] Each element of ECA identifies and informs youth-centered practices to prepare participants for an arts-based approach to learning, teaching, and performing. ECA was specifically designed as a critical community pedagogy to work in community contexts and was, in fact, developed by a community activist and literacy practitioner outside of formal educational institutions (see Anzaldúa; Boggs; Freire; hooks). In the Nuestra Voz camp, ECA worked to foster youth voice and promote collaborative learning and action. While the elements of ECA praxis elaborated upon in what follows are discussed as distinct, the framework is not linear. In other words, the categories that comprise this approach are related and not always neatly distinguishable.

Education

The first element of ECA, "Education," refers to the discussion of locally meaningful and culturally relevant topics and goals, determined in collaboration with youth and adult allies. This approach assumes youth have both something to say and to learn from each other and from their adult allies. Such an approach allows youth to participate in shaping the agenda for conversation, share distinct and even contradictory perspectives, and critically examine relevant topics.

Our camp planning committee comprised youth from the Nuestra Voz Youth Advisory Committee, members of the Crossroads Collaborative at the University of Arizona, and adult-ally directors from local youth-serving programs. Members of the committee brought ideas and research from their areas of interest and expertise to develop activities that facilitated participant engagement in the goals of the Nuestra Voz Camp. Together, we decided on three camp themes: the Ethnic Studies Ban; the School-to-Prison Pipeline; and Youth, Sexuality, Health and Rights.

The second key element of the ECA's "Education" principle is creating space for youth to be recognized as holders and producers of knowledge about these topics through their personal experiences and various ways of knowing. Because we intentionally recruited youth from several different activist organizations, the youth were able to share from their broad and distinct experiences, social locations, and perspectives. The youth participants from Kore Press's Grrls Literary Activism workshops, for instance, arrived at camp already trained to use their individual and collective voices to speak up in the public realm about injustices, including gender oppressions. The youth participants from the Eon Youth Program at Wingspan, Southern Arizona's LGBT Community Center, arrived at camp well-versed in sexual health and sexual justice.

Finally, returning Nuestra Voz program participants arrived at the summer camp with a keen understanding of race, racism, racial trauma, and racial healing due to their participation throughout the year in the racial justice programs of YWCA Tucson. In other words, each of the youth groups arrived with lived and learned knowledges and forms of expertise that helped inform and enhance a cross-perspectival approach to the work emerging from the summer camp. We encouraged participants to share through a roundtable format that promoted group discussion.

We also collaborated with Crossroads Collaborative scholar Londie Martin and various teacher-researchers to develop a multimodal literacy activity called "I'm on the Map," which highlights the place-based, lived knowledges of youth and their spatialized practices. On this digital interactive map, youth located themselves, identified the places meaningful to them in their everyday lives, and highlighted the places in which they were involved in change-oriented projects. It offered an opportunity for the development of relational literacies, or those practices that can make youth visible, knowable, and understandable to one another, and allowed participants to realize that youth from across multiple community contexts were involved in related change-oriented activities. Through the "I'm on the Map" activity, participants co-developed a critical awareness of other places and practices across the Tucson community.

Connection

"Connection," the second element of ECA, refers to the opportunities youth participants are given to explore how the youth-identified and -developed camp topics are connected to one another across distinctions in race, class, gender, sexuality, education, and immigrant status. Participants worked through activities designed to challenge them to creatively identify connections between the topics, themselves, and their communities. It is through the "Connection" component that participants began to see themselves and their individual and community histories as meaningful and relevant. They began to identify not only as agents of local histories, but of social change as well.[3]

For example, to encourage youths' analytical connections between personal stories and broader histories of the topics, we created an "historic timeline" for youth to help populate, a practice we learned at the Gay-Straight Alliance Advocacy and Youth Leadership Academy held in Sacramento, CA. We used butcher paper along a wall to map out the international, national, local, and personal timeline of a topic, inviting consideration of the multiple relationships between events along these temporal and geographic axes. This timeline included major events in the world, in the United States, in the state of Arizona, and in the lives of youth participants that we discussed as a whole group. Youth were encouraged to identify and reflect on how their experiences correlated with broader historic events. This exercise not only helped youth to connect their individual lives to world events, it made them legible as social and historic actors in a local context.

To foster awareness of connections between overlapping systems of injustice, exclusion, and oppression, we additionally provided a tool to youth participants that was informed by the work of Critical Race theorist, Mari Matsuda, and moved them to consider "asking the other question." Participants used the "other question" approach throughout the camp to first identify racism in a given context and then to see if, through critical inquiry (asking different questions about the same contexts), participants could also identify sexism, classism, and/or heterosexism. In this way, participants were encouraged to consider multiple perspectives and actively relate across differences to collaborate in projects for social justice. They also learned the importance of carefully constructing questions from multiple perspectives within the practice of critical inquiry.

Action

ECA's final component, "Action," refers to understanding the unique power of young people to address social justice issues in their communities. "Action" provides a space for youth to interpret their work as activism, to brainstorm and create art that uses their talents to support change, and to develop a perspective about "Action" that conveys both short- and long-term goals. Numerous examples of youth- and adult-ally created art activism served to inspire, encourage and model "Action." At the camp, participants developed groups around a focus topic and worked intensively on creating a project that was presented to a community audience of other youth, adults, family members, invited city officials, and supporters of the YWCA.

Participants chose to center our "Action" efforts on media literacy and civic and arts activism in the context of social marketing (see Duncan-Andrade). Youth were presented with definitions and examples of social and corporate marketing to consider the various ways in which marketing techniques are used to persuade, educate, and encourage change.[4] In small groups, youth viewed specific social marketing campaigns and discussed questions such as: What behavior is the ad targeting? What change are they asking the viewer to make? Who is their target audience? Who created the ad? Print media, DIY videos, and guerilla media styles were examined to show a wide range of possibilities, and to address the ways in which community-based social marketing can be utilized—particularly when access to technology is limited.

The social marketing approach was intended to teach youth about the rhetorical framing of media messages: Participants learned about the context within which a message is created, the role of the author/s, and the idea of "audience." Three groups formed around the camp themes of Ethnic Studies, the School-to-Prison Pipeline, and Youth, Sexuality, Health, and Rights. In whole-group discussions, youth explored how these topic areas were similar and dissimilar. We recognized that one commonality across the three topics was the restriction youth experienced in terms of access to knowledge and resources, and action projects addressed this restriction. Youth produced media from their own perspectives and social locations (see Henry Jenkins, 2007, on participatory culture and media education), through art forms including writing, spoken word, video production, and photography.

Group One: A Focus on Ethnic Studies

The group focusing on Ethnic Studies decided to address the violent and often racist language used in online comments (see Baym)[5] in response to local newspaper stories referencing Ethnic Studies debates in Tucson. They discussed the different ways in which they and their peers had experienced the efforts to ban Ethnic Studies, and noted their frustration at receiving negative messages and threats, in addition to being dismissed or ignored by adults in decision-making roles and other seats of power. Youth found that anonymous commenters expressed more discursive violence online, particularly when discussing issues of immigration and race.

Building on what they had learned about community-based social marketing, the group launched a mini-campaign around the slogan, "Online Comments Don't Stay Online." With this video, the group hoped to inform the community about the negative effects of violent language used to frame the debate and its possible correlation to verbal and physical threats made against youth in their efforts to save Ethnic Studies. Their video short highlighted the hostile online media climate that was created around the Ethnic Studies debates, and how it permeated their lives as students and as family and community members.

Group Two: A Focus on the School-to-Prison Pipeline

The second group addressed the school-to-prison pipeline and zero-tolerance sentencing policies, using the media of stop motion photography and animation to create a short video. They worked to intervene in the predominant rhetorical framing of youth as disinterested in their education, unmotivated, criminal, and as predestined failures. Together with adult allies, youth researched statistics about bullying and the various forms of discrimination youth from diverse backgrounds experience in school. They also considered the consequences of being educated in schools with a police presence and harsh consequences for minor infractions. They found creative ways to educate one another on the statistics and labels that negatively affect young people. The video calls for youth, adults, and the greater community to reimagine youth as interested, motivated, and capable. Ultimately, their creative work calls on community members to take action to make schools safer, more productive, and a meaningful learning environment for all young people.

Group Three: A Focus on Sex Ed

The third group focused on the *de facto* practice of abstinence-only education in Arizona schools. They discussed the consequences of abridged access to information on sexual health and healthy sexualities. They learned about recent legislation, termed the Parents' Bill of Rights, that required parental permission for students' participation in sexual education courses, and simultaneously established the right for parents to opt their students out of any class with sexual content. They expressed the need, as did youth in the Ethnic Studies group, for curriculum to be relevant to their lives, and for a broad youth population to be represented in their curricula.

These youth expressed the desire to learn more about how to have healthy interpersonal relationships. They confronted the harsh realities of not having access to the knowledge that they knew they needed to be sexually and relationally healthy. Informed by the principles of community-based social marketing, this group decided to create a public service announcement for viewing by other camp participants and a public audience at the end of the camp, and for use by the Crossroads Collaborative. They interviewed one another about their experiences in sex education classes: some students had not had sex education; some had had abstinence-only health classes. Others had received comprehensive sexuality education at the Eon Youth Lounge.

Their conversations strategically employed the toolbox the planning committee had prepared, which included information about safe sex, as well as local and national statistics concerning youth sexual health. Youth drew damaging statistics on their bodies and added storytelling pieces from the interviews they conducted with one another to illustrate diverse perspectives and damaging consequences of youth experience with abstinence-only education. This creative approach served as a strategy to disrupt deficit-driven (limited and limiting) understandings of youth and their needs (see Solórzano & Yosso); to focus on the ill effects of abstinence-only education; and to intervene in practices that rendered all LGBTQ students, and any sexually active students, invisible in abstinence-only educational contexts. Additionally, and as an act we've come to understand as a literacy remix, they re-distributed speaking parts that situated them outside their own identities throughout the video (see Jenkins et al. on participatory culture and remixed media). For example, one student might speak on behalf of a transgender participant but not necessarily identify as transgender. This accomplished a kind of coalitional approach to the making of their PSA. By remixing stories, youth effectively disconnected bodies from their particular narratives to challenge dominant cultural logics (and their regulating powers) in order to produce images of youth as subjects who desire knowledge/s and claim the right to access them, produce them, and teach them (see Butler).[6]

The critical and creative work that youth generated at camp functioned rhetorically to intervene in deficit-driven stories and statistics that produce misunderstandings of youth and their lived contexts. Camp participants chose to produce slam poetry and video performances to address the intersections of their identities, experiences, and social locations. Through these productions, youth expressed an understanding that they were being kept from pursuing particular knowledges and resources. They believed that many adults in the community had low estimations of their abilities and potentials. They collectively questioned how it is possible to move through a system of formal education and still lack the knowledge needed to make informed and healthy choices about their lives.

Evidence of the successful integration of the "action" component of ECA included youths' self-presentation as holders and producers of knowledge; their coalitional efforts; their expanded understanding of connections across types of oppression; and their ultimate actions to change something in the world. Youth creatively and confidently integrated their lived knowledges and experiences with new knowledges, and spoke with confidence and conviction about their needs. Spoken word and slam poetry have become sites and practices for youth from diverse locations in Tucson to continue to express and to take action on their shared needs, dreams, and desires.

ECA for Community / Academic Collaborations: Possibilities, Limitations, and Implications

In creating a space in which youth experienced themselves and their communities as important and informative, and in facilitating youth voice and advocating for the rights of youth to engage in social issues that impact them and their communities, the Nuestra Voz summer camp succeeded in meeting its objectives. Youth participated in a practice of relational and remixed literacies when they made themselves legible to one another by sharing life stories and deeply held interests. In learning from one another, and allowing that learning to inform broader inquiry, all participants—youth and adult allies alike—engaged in a generative reciprocity of teaching and of research. Adults learned, or were reminded, that youth care about themselves, one another, their schools, homes, and communities.

Pre-surveys and post-surveys, designed and developed by youth and adult participants and members of the Crossroads Collaborative, also suggest the effectiveness of the ECA approach we engaged at the camp. Pre-surveys revealed that youth arrived feeling "sad," "frustrated," and "angry," as well as with a clear desire to better understand both passed and pending legislation in Arizona. They also wanted to learn about how to respond to issues they considered relevant to their lives in a way that was meaningful, effective, and that would be heard and seriously considered—especially by those in positions to facilitate change. Post-surveys indicated that participants learned that the broad issues the camp addressed were connected and mutually relevant; that they had a right to use their voices and visions to express needs, interests, dreams, and desires; and that art can serve as a tool for education and activism. They reported feeling "passionate" about change and "determined" to participate in their schools and communities—particularly around the right to comprehensive knowledge and information.

While these camp successes were significant, there were also challenges to implementing and collaborating within the ECA framework—particularly in the camp's one-week timeframe. One challenge that we had not anticipated was the arrival of already-formed groups of young people. It was a challenge to encourage participants out of the groups they were first affiliated with—even though the work that was ultimately produced expressed strong coalitional potential. With more time, and perhaps better-developed strategies, we can imagine a more robust mixing of youth participants across creative productions and performances.

While we understand that there are elements of the camp that cannot be replicated across distinct contexts, we do believe there is much here that can inform related efforts. Literacy practitioners in many situations may be able to draw from ECA principles to create effective learning and action communities. ECA's first principle of "Education" calls for the participation of learners in the selection of content, and the honoring of learners as holders and producers of knowledge, concepts that can be implemented through practices such as advisory councils. The concept of "Connection" draws attention to the need for coalitional work. Collaborations can be designed to explicitly encourage participants to connect across social spaces and identifications, learning how to organize themselves toward critical inquiry and creative collaborations. ECA's final principle, "Action," allows participants the space to empower each other to co-present their projects and knowledges about social justice to one another and to the greater community.

When Alexia Vazquez' and Enrique Garcia's poem, "No More Ignorant Love," was performed at the community event concluding the camp, youth voice was made audible. The performance served as a reminder that there is much to learn from youth whose own lives are expressions of lived knowledges and lived desires. The production and performance of the poem became a form of youth community action. When youth are supported to bring their lived and learned knowledges together, they learn to use their voices to tell about their lives (and so their histories), to teach, and to call for needed change as an expression of informed action.

Camp youth emerged as critical and creative peer educators and collaborators fully capable of participating in the civic realm and of making themselves legible and recognizable to one another as allies in broad-based social justice work. Youth called on their formal and experiential literacies—including academic, community, and family literacies—to craft creative participatory media productions addressing injustices and inequities in Tucson and beyond.

Acknowledgments

The authors wish to thank Tucson youth for their work and collaborations to plan, facilitate, and create the productions and performances we consider here. We thank Stephen T. Russell and Brenda O. Daly for their helpful reviews and comments on early drafts of our manuscript and Leah Stauber for her editorial assistance. We offer special thanks to Rachael Wendler for her support, wisdom, and insightful suggestions. Finally, we would like to thank the Ford Foundation for their generous support.

Endnotes

1. Prior to the collaboration, Gonzales worked with local middle and high school students in Tucson for a three-year focus on race, racism, racial trauma, and racial healing through performance. Licona had just finished work on her book on zines, or self-published magazines: Zines in Third Space: Radical Cooperation and Borderlands Rhetorics. In the book, Licona explores the counter-cultural productions and coalitional potentials and practices of queer and queer-of-color zinesters or zine authors.

2. Licona's work as a critical feminist pedagogue is further informed by a Funds of Knowledge approach to learning contexts, the principles of place-based pedagogy, and the concept of critical localism (see Stephen Goldzwig; Norma Gonzáles, Luis Moll, and Cathy Amanti). In terms of community literacies, these concepts are connected to Goldblatt's belief that we should be actively aware of the real problems faced by everyday members of the communities in which we live (see Eli Goldblatt).

3. Principles of radical and feminist pedagogies together with LatCrit and Critical Race Theory (CRT), as well as literatures in youth action research, inform our understanding of participants as agents of local histories and social change. On radical pedagogy, see Elizabeth Ellsworth; Henry Giroux and Peter McLaren; and Carmen Luke. On youth action research, especially relevant to our local context, see Julio Cammarota and Michelle Fine.

4. Gonzales draws from the work of Doug McKenzie-Mohr and William Smith in *Fostering Sustainable Behavior: An Introduction to Community-based Social Marketing* (2011) to inform her approach to social marketing as a practice that puts broad notions of societal benefit over profit.

5. The process and practice of "extremely argumentative communication," understood as "messages that include swearing, insults, name calling, negative affect, and typographic energy," is also called flaming, and is highlighted in the work of Nancy Baym, who focuses her attentions on social networking sites, SNS, and other social media (Personal Connections in the Digital Age, 57).

6. Licona is at work developing and connecting concepts of remixed and relational knowledges and literacies to community practice, participatory media production, and subcultural contexts. She is interested in the potential of such remixes to disrupt notions of the exceptional or "deserving" youth and sees such a strategy as potentially coalitional (see Karma Chávez' forthcoming work on coalitional possibilities). Relational literacies, related to Licona's work on community literacies and relational knowledges, is a concept named and taken up explicitly in Londie Martin's

2013 dissertation titled "The Spatiality of Queer Youth Activism: Sexuality and the Performance of Relational Literacies through Multimodal Play."

Works Cited

Anzaldúa, Gloria. Ed. *Making Face, Making Soul/Haciendo Caras: Creative and Critical Perspectives by Feminists of Color.* San Francisco: Aunt Lute, 1990. Print.
Basu, Kaustuv. "The Next Target?" Inside Higher Ed, April 17, 2012. Web. 1 July 2013.
Boggs, Grace Lee. *The Next American Revolution: Sustainable Activism for the 21st Century.* Berkeley: University of California Press, 2012. Print.
Butler, Judith. *Gender Trouble.* New York: Routledge Classics, 2006. Print
Cammarota, Julio. "A Social Justice Approach to Achievement: Guiding Latina/o Students toward Educational Attainment with a Challenging, Socially Relevant Curriculum." *Equity & Excellence in Education* 40 (2007): 87–96. Print.
Cammarota, Julio, and Michelle Fine. *Revolutionizing Education: Youth Participatory Action Research.* New York: Routledge, 2008. Print.
Chávez, Karma R., "Counter-Public Enclaves and Understanding the Function of Rhetoric in Social Movement Coalition-Building." *Communication Quarterly* 59.1 (2011):1-18. Print.
———. *Queer Migration Politics: Activist Rhetoric and Coalitional Possibilities.* Urbana: University of Illinois Press, (in press).
Delgado Bernal, Dolores. "Critical Race Theory, Latino Critical Theory, and Critical Raced-Gendered Epistemologies: Recognizing Students of Color as Holders and Creators of knowledge. *Qualitative Inquiry* 8 (2002):105-26. Print.
Duncan-Andrade, Jeff. "Urban Youth, Media Literacy, and Increased Critical
Civic Participation." *Beyond Resistance! Youth Activism and Community Change: New Democratic Possibilities for Practice and Policy for America's Youth.* Ed. Shawn Ginwright. Pedro Noguera, and Julio Cammarota. New York, Routledge, 2006. 149-170. Print.
Ellsworth, Elizabeth. "Why Doesn't This Feel Empowering? Working Through Repressive Myths of Critical Pedagogy." *Feminisms and Critical Pedagogy.* Ed. Carmen Luke and Jennifer Gore. New York: Routledge, 1992. 90-119. Print.
Finley, Susan. "Critical Arts-Based Inquiry: The Pedagogy and Performance of a Radical Ethical Aesthetic. *The Sage Handbook of Qualitiative Research.* Ed. Norman K. Denzin and Yvonna S. Lincoln. Los Angeles: Sage, 2011. 435-450. Print.
Freire, Paulo. *Pedagogy of the Oppressed.* Trans. Myra Bergman Ramos. New York: Continuum Books, 1993. Print.
———. *Pedagogy of Hope: Reliving Pedagogy of the Oppressed.* New York: Bloomsbury Academic, 2004. Print.
Giroux, Henry and McLaren Peter. "Radical Pedagogy as Cultural Politics: Beyond the Discourse of Critique and Anti-Utopianism." *Theory/Pedagogy/Politics: Texts for Change.* Ed. Donald Morton and Mas'ud Zavarzadeh. Urbana: University of Illinois Press, 1991. 152-186. Print.
Goldblatt, Eli. *Because We Live Here: Sponsoring Literacy Beyond the College Curruciculum.* Cresskill: Hampton Press, 2007. Print.

Gonzáles, Norma, Luis Moll, and Cathy Amanti. *Funds of Knowledge: Theorizing Practices in Households, Communities, and Classrooms*. New Jersey: Lawrence Erlbaum, 2005. Print.

Herdt, Gilbert. *Moral Panics, Sex Panics: Fear and the Fight over Sexual Rights*. New York: New York University Press, 2009. Print.

hooks, bell. *Teaching to Transgress*. New York: Routledge, 1994. Print.

Jenkins, Henry, Ravi Purushotma, Margaret Weigel, Katie Clinton and Alice J. Robison. "Confronting the Challenges of Participatory Culture - Media Education for the 21st Century (Part Two)." *Digital Kompetanse: Nordic Journal of Digital Literacy* 2 (2007): 97-113. Web. 1 July 2013.

Licona, Adela C. *Zines in Third Space: Radical Cooperation and Borderlands Rhetoric*. Albany: State University of New York Press, 2012. Print.

Licona, Adela C., Stephen T. Russell, and the Crossroads Collaboration. "Teachers-Researchers in Engaged Transdisciplinary Public Scholarship: The Mixed and Messy Practices of Critical and Creative Inquiry." Manuscript in preparation. 2013.

Luke, Carmen. "Feminist Politics in Radical Pedagogy." *Feminisms and Critical Pedagogy*. Ed. Carmen Luke and Jennifer Gore. New York: Routledge, 1992. 25-53. Print.

Martin, Londie. The Spatiality of Queer Youth Activism: Sexuality and the Performance of Relational Literacies through Multimodal Play. Unpublished dissertation. University of Arizona, 2013. Print.

Matsuda, Mari J. "Beside My Sister, Facing the Enemy: Legal Theory Out of Coalition." Stanford Law Review 43.6 (1991): 1183-92. Print.

McKenzie-Mohr, Doug, and William Smith. *Fostering Sustainable Behavior: An Introduction to Community-based Social Marketing*. New Society Publishers, 2011. Print.

Mitchell, Gordon R. "Public Argument Action Research and the Learning Curve of New Social Movements." *Argumentation and Advocacy* 40 (2004): 209-225. Print.

Planas, Roque. "Arizona Official Considers Targeting Mexican American Studies in University." Fox News Latino, March 28, 2012. Web. 1 July 2013.

Solórzano, Daniel G., and Tara J. Yosso. "From Racial Stereotyping and Deficit Discourse Toward a Critical Race Theory in Teacher Education." *Multicultural Education* 9 (2001): 2-8. Print.

Adela C. Licona, Ph.D., is associate professor in Rhetoric, Composition, and the Teaching of English and co-director of the Crossroads Collaborative at the University of Arizona (aclicona@email.arizona.edu).

J. Sarah Gonzales is founder of national social justice consulting company TruthSarita, LLC and co-director of Spoken Futures, Inc. (sarah@truthsarita.com).

Empower Latino Youth (ELAYO): Leveraging Youth Voice to Inform the Public Debate on Pregnancy, Parenting and Education

Elodia Villaseñor, Miguel Alcalá, Ena Suseth Valladares, Miguel A. Torres, Vanessa Mercado, and Cynthia A. Gómez

Youth perspectives are routinely absent from research and policy initiatives. This article presents a project that infuses youth participation, training and mentorship into the research process and teaches youth how to become policy advocates. Empower Latino Youth (ELAYO) studies the individual and systemic factors impacting sexuality and childbearing among Latino youth and seeks to reduce negative stereotypes and elevate the social standing of Latino youth. As a team-in-training, ELAYO provides adolescents, undergraduate and graduate students the opportunity to develop research skills while learning the importance of linking science to policy. This paper was developed in collaboration with Latino youth.

> *We're searching for new ways to discover and change identities imposed on us and illustrating our strengths and capabilities.*
>
> —ELAYO Youth Advisory Group Member

The Issue

Latino[1] youth are the fastest growing ethnic group in the United States and are disproportionately impacted by unplanned pregnancies, HIV and other sexually transmitted infection (STI) rates, as compared to their European-American counterparts (California Adolescent Sexual Health Work Group; California Department of Public Health; Centers for Disease Control and Prevention 2). Prior research has attributed these disparities to factors such as earlier onset of sexual activity, lack of family communication around sexuality, inconsistent use of condoms or contraception, gender inequality in sexual relationships and cultural/ religious beliefs (Afable-Munsuz and Brindis; Cox; Guilamo-Ramos et al.). The dominant discourse in addressing sexuality, reproductive health, and adolescent childbearing among the Latino community approaches these issues from a deficit perspective. In so doing, Latino youth and their families are blamed, as individuals, for their "choices" and "conditions." Discourse from a deficit perspective has led to the continued vilification of youth, with labels of "hyper-sexuality" and "irresponsibility." This unfounded criticism often leads to punitive measures for pregnant and parenting youth, including systemic discrimination within educational institutions, such as pressure to transfer out of comprehensive high schools into alternative programs, and being subjected to substandard education

(California Latinas for Reproductive Justice 6). In segregating pregnant and parenting youth, opportunities to graduate, prepare for college and other economic advances are often hampered. This is one example of how the use of a deficit lens, and blaming the individual, devisibilizes structural inequities, perpetuating stereotypes and further marginalizing the Latino community. In fact, the deficit lens not only addresses disparities on an individual level, it negates the sociopolitical undercurrents at play, including anti-immigrant legislation (Ayón and Gaddy).

The Ford Foundation's Youth Sexuality, Reproductive Health and Rights Initiative recognizes that most sexual and reproductive health programs ignore the broader sociocultural and economic factors that prevent young people from making healthy decisions, and that contribute to their vulnerability to poor sexual and reproductive health outcomes. Through grant support, the Foundation provided an opportunity for our academic-community partnership to engage Latino youth in research, training and strategic communication efforts. As they have noted, "many young people are also denied access to information and support that would enable them to protect their own sexual and reproductive health" (see: http://www.fordfoundation.org/issues/sexuality-and-reproductive-health-and-rights/youth-sexuality-reproductive-health-and-rights). We believe, therefore, that the greatest opportunity for change lies in creating a context where Latino youth can learn more about the issues they are reported to be facing; can give voice to their own experiences; and, together with academic and community partners, can create effective research and communications efforts that inform policies and programs. Engaging Latino youth as equal partners in knowledge-seeking and advocacy for fair and just policies empowers them to become our future leaders.

This paper describes our process for Latino youth engagement—for giving power to youth voice—and is a process that is still *in progress*. These descriptions and stories represent our work-to-date, and have been created in close partnership with youth currently participating in the ELAYO: Empower Latino Youth Project.

ELAYO: **E**mpower **La**tino **Yo**uth Project

As a Ford Foundation grantee in the Youth Sexuality, Reproductive Health and Rights Initiative, the Health Equity Institute at San Francisco State University and California Latinas for Reproductive Justice embarked on a unique project: Empower Latino Youth (ELAYO). This project incorporates research, training, and mentorship as key elements of an alternative educational pipeline. Strategic communication plays a pivotal role within ELAYO's activities by enabling

Figure 1. First ELAYO Youth Advisory Group Meeting, February 2011

public discourse about sexual and reproductive health and rights through innovative communication strategies that translate science to inform practice and policy. These strategies include the production of documentaries focused on Latino youth's sexual and reproductive health needs; educating policymakers through formal briefings with California legislative staff; the production of Community Briefs which translate research findings into accessible knowledge for communities; and offering Community Science Dialogues in which providers, researchers, teachers and youth can all come together to discuss the topic, view a documentary, or discuss particular findings from the ELAYO project. Although the three primary elements of ELAYO are research, training and strategic communication, each component is fluid, with each influencing the other and the overall goal of the Project: to create a paradigm shift that positions Latino youth sexuality within an asset-based framework.

The methodology used for research in ELAYO was mixed-methods, incorporating interviews, focus groups, and surveys among Latino youth and key adult stakeholders in both urban and agricultural regions of California to increase our understanding of how Latino youth balance competing cultural and social values regarding sexuality, parenting and education. Also assessed were youths' knowledge of their sexual and reproductive health and rights, and how these might vary for Latino youth who have become parents. As the Community partner, California Latinas for Reproductive Justice (CLRJ) ensures that ELAYO is strongly rooted in a reproductive justice framework. CLRJ also ensures that research is translated to inform and shape California reproductive and sexual health laws and policies that affect pregnant and parenting youth, through the development of policy recommendations based on key findings. Research outcomes are currently being analyzed for future dissemination. This paper focuses on the processes of our work and how youth voices were integral to the project, while also highlighting the role of partnerships and collaborations.

A University-Community Partnership

The Health Equity Institute (HEI) at San Francisco State University and California Latinas for Reproductive Justice (CLRJ) joined together to create a university-community   partnership to address the sexual health and rights of Latino youth in California. CLRJ is a statewide policy and advocacy organization whose mission is to advance California Latinas'/os' reproductive health and rights within a social-justice and human-rights framework. Given the critical need to reframe the political, academic and social discourse surrounding the sexuality of young Latinos, one of CLRJ's program areas promotes systemic policy change that directly advances their needs, interests and voices. Together, HEI and CLRJ conceptualized the initial project focus, defined each of their roles on the project, and co-wrote the grant application that ultimately led to receipt of the Ford Foundation award.

In addition to facilitating trainings (described below), collaborating on data analysis and publications, and leading the policy efforts for ELAYO, CLRJ also extended an invitation to one of the Youth Advisory Group members to travel to Los Angeles from San Francisco to see first-hand how research informs policy, and how it can be translated into action. The HEI senior investigator (Gómez), ELAYO's project director (Villaseñor), CLRJ's director of research (Suseth Valladares) and relevant CLRJ senior administrators continue to meet quarterly to review the progress of the project and to continuously ensure coordination and clarification of roles and responsibilities. Together, we continue to ensure that youth voices are present in all of our activities.

The Important Role of Youth Voices

By incorporating youth voices, ELAYO seeks to contribute to a dialogue that shifts Latino public-health discourse to an asset-based framework, providing a necessary positive rhetoric for those who will shape our future: youth. The sentiment expressed by one of the Youth Advisory Group members early on still resonates: "I want (to be a part of ELAYO) because I am Latino and I am part of the community and I would like to be informed." This statement can be broken down into four parts 1) The desire to become engaged, 2) pride in racial and cultural identity 3) identifying with a larger community, and 4) desire to become informed.

After many hours of working with youth, it has become easy for us to see this statement come to life and resonate for many of them. First, the "engagement" portion of the statement speaks to an eagerness for becoming a part of something—creating positive change. Second, it has been shown that pride in racial and cultural identity serve as protective factors for Latino youth (Denner). Third, having a strong positive identification with a community is a protective factor: community fosters a sense of security and commonality between families, or similar groups of persons, such as LGBTQ youth or young parents, leading to a sense of belonging that serves as a protective factor (Denner). Lastly, the need to be informed indicates a need for reciprocity—not only will the team-in-training learn from the youth, but the youth can learn from the team, making knowledge production fluid and bidirectional. The learning model established within ELAYO embraces Shor and Freire's notion of "liberation education," which acknowledges the indispensable roles of action, critical reflection, curiosity, demanding inquiry, uneasiness, etc. Thus the team, from high school students to senior investigator, together become critical agents in the act of knowing (Shor and Freire). Through becoming a part of not only the research process, but also the training, policy briefings and overall strategic communication process, and using a strength-based approach, "young people may thrive and civil society may prosper" (Lerner et al. 15). Youth can create change through research and action, and, perhaps, become the next generation of social science researchers and/or policymakers.

Youth Engagement in ELAYO

> *I am a passionate and driven Latino. I am a part of ELAYO because it creates a space that empowers Latinos and creates opportunities.*
>
> —YAG member

Figure 2. ELAYO YAG members join staff and Dr. Gómez at national convening of Ford Foundation Grantees in January, 2012

The Youth Advisory Group (YAG) was developed with the intention to foster the growth of future social scientists and sexuality researchers, encouraging and supporting matriculation to higher education while also informing, participating and contributing youth voice to the research process. To address the goal of creating a type of educational pipeline that promotes higher education, four high school students—two female sophomores and two male juniors—were initially recruited. Four undergraduate students from San Francisco State University (SF State) were also recruited (three females and one male). Recruitment occurred through various youth-serving community organizations in San Francisco, and among San Francisco State University contacts initiated by ELAYO staff's personal and professional networks. The recruitment process included many phone calls to agencies, as well as in-person conversations about the research and training aspects of the Project. A $25 stipend was provided to each YAG member for each meeting attended and, since meetings were held in the evening, dinner became a part of the agenda. YAG members often made requests for subsequent meeting times and food options, allowing for different tastes and opinions to be honored.

The YAG meetings are facilitated by research staff-in-training (one post-baccalaureate Latino male and one post-MPH Latina female). The process of unifying the Youth Advisory Group began with getting to know each other (through "ice breaker" activities), establishing ground rules, and writing and signing a contract, "YAG Rights and Responsibilities." YAG meetings began with introductions and check-ins, along with eating and interaction time, since the meetings were held in the evenings during traditional dinner time to allow all persons to attend after school and work commitments. Over the course of 15 months, YAG members and core staff gathered for 10 meetings, four trainings and one national Grantee Convening where all current grantees, representing diverse geographic regions from the Ford Foundation's Initiative on Youth, Sexuality, Health, and Rights, were gathered. The content and function of trainings and meetings are elaborated in more detail below.

Youth who participated in the advisory group joined with different levels of knowledge, responsibility and engagement. As group facilitators, it was crucial for us to honor the starting point of all members. From there, a foundation of trust and safe space emerged as the key to ensuring positive group formation. The YAG, as a group, demonstrated support and flexibility for all of its members. For example, when childcare was an issue, younger siblings or children were allowed to remain in the room while meetings took place. Similarly, when a new youth member was hesitant to attend alone, she was allowed to attend the meeting with a friend. In the latter example, by the third meeting, this young person not only attended by herself, but was also more outspoken and willing to participate without prompting.

Youth Participatory Research

The engagement of Latino youth in all processes of research, the dissemination of research findings, and action through policy advocacy are modeled on Youth Participatory Action Research. Youth Participatory Action Research is rooted in several fields, including, Community Based Participatory Research (CBPR) and empowerment evaluation and positive youth development (Powers and Tiffany). Youth are able to acquire skills, gain knowledge, and challenge themselves. According to Powers and Tiffany, youth developmental assets acquired or enhanced through participatory research include leadership skills as change agents; critical thinking ability; and the development of diverse social networks and a broad knowledge base. Other valuable skills acquired through participatory research include writing; analysis; effective presentation and advocacy; decision making; and the formation of new relationships with adults and community members. These youth serve as role models to other youth, and become experts possessing local knowledge about issues that affect youth. A recent study found that youth participation in YPAR was associated with adolescents' increases in socio-political skills and motivation to influence their schools and communities (Ozer and Douglas). The acquisition of these assets empowers youth to create social change.

Our process follows many of the principles of community-based participatory research (CBPR) (Israel et al.). Though ELAYO is not strictly a CBPR project, the involvement of youth in the advisory group, as well as students in various stages of their educational trajectory working as staff on ELAYO, has: 1) created social support systems (ex: within the youth advisory group itself, between youth involved in the Ford Foundation Sexuality Initiative grantee projects, and ELAYO staff); 2) allowed for the learning of research tools (ex: interview and focus group tool development); 3) gained skills that may be employable (ex: how to facilitate a focus group or conduct an interview); 4) expanded youths' ability to view inequities holistically through a reproductive justice lens (ex: include analysis of the economic, social, and political power and resources available to communities and the choices that are generated as a result) and, 5) involved youth in the production of knowledge (ex: collaborating on articles such as this one). These components are all infused into ELAYO to strengthen its process by not only creating a richer deepening of knowledge within the specific fields of sexual health and rights and Latino populations and educational equity, but also providing opportunity and context for the Latino youth involved.

Reflection: From Undergraduate University Student to ELAYO Staff

I began working on this project at the tail end of my time as an undergraduate student at San Francisco State University. My first task as a student assistant was to read the literature on the issues ELAYO hoped to tackle: Latino youth sexual and reproductive health and rights. My experience in research had been limited to an introduction to research course that I took as an undergraduate student. Working on ELAYO has broadened my understanding of qualitative and quantitative research. The skills that I have gained as a research assistant range from learning how to do a literature review, to interview and focus group facilitation. And they continue to grow as we are immersed in data analyses.

Prior to joining the ELAYO Project, I had only planned on graduating with my BA in Psychology and jumping into a career in Counseling. There wasn't much thought of furthering my education. Now, after working with individuals that have gone to get their Master's and PhDs, continuing my education is something that is embedded into my future plans. I have had the opportunity to speak with individuals who have studied at San Francisco State University, University of California at Berkeley, and even, University of Michigan at Ann Arbor.

Not only is graduate school in my radar but also, continuing my career in research is something that I plan on doing. Being a part of a project that directly impacts my community and family has given me a lens into how I want to change the inequalities that impact Latino youth today and tomorrow.

Training Sessions

> *I love them (trainings)! Sometimes I wish there was more time for more in depth conversations and to look at topics concerning us.*
>
> —YAG member

One of the three pillars of ELAYO is the training component. Intended to facilitate the professional growth and development of the team, training sessions took place to coincide with the various phases of the Project. The training sessions were designed for both the core ELAYO research team-in-training and the YAG. Since the background and experience of team members and YAG members were so varied, the training sessions were a place for everyone to gain exposure and contribute their expertise to the topic at hand. Often, the presentation themes resonated with core members of ELAYO and youth alike. Table 1 illustrates the array of trainings that were provided to the YAG and core research team-in-training.

The first training session was conducted by Dr. Cynthia A. Gómez, the senior investigator on the project, on the topic of "Sexuality, Health and Latinos." The training provided an overview for the ELAYO team and YAG members on Latino sexual-health related statistics and the deficit models of Latino youth sexuality, reproductive health, and childbearing that ELAYO was created to counteract. YAG members were highly engaged, asking questions, sharing personal stories, and requesting additional research articles to read to become better informed about the issues. It was evident that youth were capable of integrating knowledge that is not often available to them, or is perceived as "too academic" for a youth audience.

Table 1: Training Sessions Delivered to Youth and/or Research Team-in-Training

When	Topic
Spring, 2011	Sexuality, Health & Latinos
Spring, 2011	Policy, Advocacy & Reproductive Justice
Spring, 2011	Educational Equity and Latino Youth
Summer, 2011	Qualitative tool development (Focus group guide, interview guide)
Summer, 2011	Basics on Focus Groups & Facilitation
Fall, 2011	Effective interviewing on sexual topics
Fall, 2011	Ethical Practices in Research
Fall, 2011	Incorporating Research into Documentary Films
Spring, 2012	Principles of Community-Based Participatory Research
Spring, 2012	Interpreting Qualitative Data
Spring, 2012	Survey Development
Fall, 2012	Publication Development
Spring, 2013	Interpreting Quantitative Data (Statewide Online Survey)

    CLRJ staff conducted a three-hour training, introducing the reproductive justice framework to ELAYO's research team and YAG. This training consisted of various activities and exercises intended to broaden the team's understanding of reproductive justice. One of the first activities in which the team engaged was a values-based game called, "Agree/Disagree." In this game, participants were asked to walk toward either side of the room, depending on whether they agreed or disagreed with a statement made by the facilitator regarding youth sexuality and pregnancy. Statement examples included: "All youth have the right to seek confidential reproductive and sexual health services without having to notify their parents or guardians," and "Comprehensive sexuality education should be a mandate for all public schools." Once the participants walked to their respective positions, the facilitator asked for volunteers to share why they either agreed or disagreed with the statement, allowing for respectful dialogue and debate. This activity encouraged the team, and particularly the youth, to share their own views about these issues, and to discuss how these issues affect or are perceived by their own families and communities.

    This analysis provided a way to connect with each other's stories and values, and to better understand differing viewpoints. Participants were then given a brief description and history of the related, but distinct, areas of reproductive health, reproductive rights, and reproductive justice, and the main differences within each of these advocacy movements were discussed. Due to the nature of ELAYO—with its roots in social justice, and the goal of creating a paradigm shift—addressing Youth Sexuality, Health and Rights alone was not sufficient. It was important to incorporate a reproductive justice lens prior to developing research instruments and analyzing data, because the use of this framework allows for a broader ecological view of the multiple realities of youth's lives.

This particular training was replicated with SF State students who would be creating documentary films focused on the objectives of ELAYO (see the Health and Social Justice Documentaries posted on HEI's website: www.healthequityinstitute.org) to ensure that they, too, understood the reproductive justice lens prior to developing the documentaries. These documentaries would be critical tools for creating dialogue about the sexual and reproductive needs and rights of Latino youth and their families. As part of the training, an activity called "Six Chairs" was delivered. This activity highlighted the difficulty for many in navigating the health care system. Through this activity, participants were encouraged to incorporate critical factors such as age, race, gender, class, sexual orientation, disability and immigration status when addressing reproductive and sexual health issues faced by communities of color, and, in particular, Latino youth.

Volunteers were asked to read aloud a fact and an accompanying scenario. For example, "FACT: Latinas' teen birth rate is three times higher than that of white teens." "SCENARIO: 'I am a seventeen-year-old high school junior and honor student. Now that I'm pregnant, my counselor told me I should go to a continuation school. But I'm staying at my high school because I want to graduate and go to college. My boyfriend and I got the 'abstinence only' classes. I wish we would've heard about birth control.'" The youth engaged in a discussion within which they relayed what happens to pregnant youth in their own high schools, and whether the example scenario reflected the realities in their own communities. CLRJ/HEI facilitators further asked the trainees to explore the institutional or structural barriers that prevented youth from graduating and/or preparing for college. Many of the youth commented that pregnant and parenting students seemed to be punished by the school administrators because administrators did not want other students to get pregnant; the youth expressed surprise when they were told that California and federal laws existed to prevent this type of treatment.

These trainings served multiple purposes, since they not only provided knowledge and skill-building functions, but also provided youth with a place to express their own experiences and views on issues that directly impact them on a daily basis. One young man from the YAG voiced his views that the needs of young dads were often neglected when discussing teen pregnancy. He shared with the group that his cousin's ex-girlfriend did not allow his cousin to see their son. He shared this story with the assumption that male voices would not be considered because males aren't the ones who get pregnant, and are often perceived as bad fathers. The facilitators emphasized that this is one reason why it is important to shift the way that policymakers, community members, adults involved in teenagers' upbringing, service providers, advocates and the youth themselves think about and address Latina/o youth sexuality in general, and particularly in regard to teen mothers and fathers. This case also provides a great example of how emphasizing an asset-based framework provides space for youth to feel included, share their experiences, and address the impact that stereotypes have on us all, by engaging in a deeper analysis of the issues affecting families and communities.

Though this is a brief example, the space for reflecting on lived experiences allows for critical thinking and a shared learning experience that is active. When the trainings become personal, youth continue their path towards becoming more conscious and socially transformative, and can embrace their power to create individual and social change. Future trainings will focus on data interpretation, dissemination of findings back to our local communities, and CLRJ will train and prepare the YAG and ELAYO to use these research findings to educate policymakers.

Local and National Activities of the Youth Advisory Group

In addition to the trainings that were for the personal and professional growth of the team-in-training and the YAG, formal meetings tailored specifically for YAG members also took place on a regular basis. These meetings differed from the trainings in that they were a private space for youth and their facilitators, or they focused on particular activities of contribution to the work of ELAYO. One YAG member perfectly stated what our goal for the group was: "…the YAG is a really safe place where everyone can speak their mind and not be judged." The partnership built between the team-in-training, the youth advisory group and CLRJ is one that allowed for *confianza*. The English translation of *confianza* is "confidence," but really it is much more meaningful—akin to mutual trust and support. When youth and adults can work together with *confianza,* it is then that positive transformation, development and empowerment can occur for youth and adults alike.

Some examples of the work the YAG conducted included: (1) project name development (i.e., ELAYO) and the ELAYO logo and color scheme; (2) serving as a mock focus group to provide feedback on the focus-group guide and provide critique to focus-group facilitators on their facilitation styles and skills; and (3) learning how to conduct interviews and focus groups. In the process of data collection, YAG members provided ideas for the recruitment of non-parenting and parenting youth for participation in focus groups, and also spoke with their networks about ELAYO to identify appropriate community-based organizations in the San Francisco Bay area for collaboration in recruitment of youth participants and—sometimes—space for conducting said interviews and focus groups.

One of the YAG members additionally became a part of the research team that conducted interviews and focus groups with non-parenting Latina/o youth. The interviews and focus groups were planned in a manner such that two team members were present, allowing for the YAG member to be accompanied by someone who had previously engaged in data collection. Though the roles of note-taker and facilitator alternated, the opportunity for observation and engagement remained. Experiencing the data collection process from set-up to debriefing afterwards allowed for a rich discussion that delved into what research looks like in the field during data collection. The need for additional ELAYO team members during data collection proved invaluable in allowing for greater opportunities for YAG members to engage in the process, demystifying research. In the future, meetings will include YAG input on the research analysis, interpretation of findings, and participation in the dissemination of findings and policy advocacy efforts.

Throughout our meetings, YAG members expressed an interest in being involved in every capacity of the ELAYO Project. One way ELAYO was able to expand its capacity and provide further opportunities for youth engagement and activism was by introducing Project Connect, a collaboration between four of the six grantees of the Ford Foundation Youth Sexuality, Reproductive Health and Rights Initiative. As described by the coordinator, Project Connect was a means by which youth activists connected with other youth activists across the country who were addressing issues of youth, rights and sexuality. First, we worked directly with our YAG, with curriculum provided by Project Connect, to create a two-minute video on youth participation with ELAYO. The process of creating this video far surpassed our expectations of collaboration and teamwork between the youth and staff. Though it employed a curriculum developed by Truth Sarita Consulting for Project Connect to provide the framework for video production, the actual product was entirely youth-led. The brainstorming phase was a collaborative effort by all youth involved. Three ELAYO staff were present for support and advice, but none was sought. The overall production process was safe, inviting, fun and supportive. In fact, when reminded that the scheduled end of the meeting time was quickly approaching, one youth remarked, "We don't have anywhere to go. It doesn't matter if we stay late." The message was clear: community had been built. A support system had been established. The youth took great care and pride in the production of knowledge in the form of an introductory video, "We are ELAYO." (See the video here: http://healthequity.sfsu.edu/our-work/research/elayo.html).

By sharing the videos they had created, youth were able to get a sense of the varying projects taking place throughout the country within the scope of the Ford Foundation's initiative. Not only did this further promote a sense of community within the differing youth groups, but it allowed for better understanding of different topics being addressed, creating another opportunity for dialogue. The following is an example of a response the Youth Advisory Group received,

Hey San Francisco,

Your movement on empowering Latin@ youth really touched us considering most of our communities are Latin@ as well! The safe space you guys provide remind us of our mission and made us feel as if you can make others feel completely comfortable.

With Love,

Tucson Youth Poetry Slam

ELAYO staff and youth also worked together to create a Resistance Zine. Through the curriculum, youth learned about Zines, allowing for the creation of their own contribution that shows how youth are addressing the topics within the scope of each individual Project. According to the Project Connect Zine Curriculum, a Zine is defined as a "self-published, small circulation, non-commercial booklet or magazine, usually produced by one person or a few individuals ... Zines are personal and idiosyncratic." The Zine consists of two pages from each of the four participating groups, then assembled into one product and given to the youth to distribute to their communities. In the production phase of the Zine, the youth worked diligently and asked each other questions and conducted web research about colonization, history, geography while also discussing their current educational transitions and aspirations. One can imagine the additional possibilities for creativity, dialogue and the sharing of expertise that arises from such an exciting collaboration.

Figure 3. The final Zine from ELAYO

One dynamic that was established early in the YAG meetings, and reinforced by the ELAYO alternative educational pipeline, is the bidirectional transfer of knowledge. ELAYO staff consistently checked in with each other to ensure there was not a mere "transference of existing knowledge" to students, but rather a dialogue honoring "the student's comprehension of their daily life experiences," the foundation for liberation education (Shor and Freire 67). From this reflection on life experiences, not only was critical thinking promoted, but so too was the act of learning from one's own lived experience. Students learned to deconstruct reality, becoming more conscious and empowered to make individual and social change. We realized that the students had achieved this level of consciousness and empowerment when one YAG member stated, "(I can) take this knowledge and use it when discussing about politics in school and outside of school..." In essence, this is the power of ELAYO; YAG members demonstrated incredible aptitude to not only express themselves, but to act as agents of change.

Self-Evaluation and Reflections of Youth Participants

I am an open-minded and family oriented Latina. I am a part of ELAYO because I want to change the perspective of Latinos.

—YAG member

Throughout the course of the first year, the YAG members were asked to engage in one evaluation and three written reflections. The evaluation included questions such as: What made you decide to participate in the Youth Advisory Group? How do you feel about the trainings and meetings so far? Is there something else you would like to learn that we haven't covered yet in the meetings or trainings? What are your goals and aspirations for the future? Have you considered being a researcher or exploring the topics we have covered in the meetings and trainings in the future?

Figure 4.

These self-evaluations and reflections were a way for the ELAYO staff to provide a venue for YAG members to express anything they may have not had the opportunity or felt comfortable to say during the meetings. As time went on, and our time together grew, their reflections began to change. The youth participants felt as though they could simply speak their minds, so that everyone in the group knew how they felt. As one YAG member stated, "It's really fun for me because I get to meet new people and just say what's on my mind and it's a good experience for me because I'm usually a shy person but after a while it goes away." At times, their reflections and self-evaluations became a group discussion. In a matter of months, we went from being complete strangers to viewing each other as family.

Through these writings and discussions, we were able to learn how the topics YAG members discussed gave them the confidence to be leaders amongst their peers and within their communities They also expressed a desire to continue to learn about research, and their interest in attending a university for undergraduate and graduate work grew. At present, the ELAYO staff feels that we have been able to provide a safe space for the youth to grow and to be themselves. The exploration of these topics has informed the YAG process and will continue to inform how ELAYO moves forward, with input from all team members.

Lessons Learned

Though the ELAYO Project is not over, we have already noticed that time constraints pose challenges with respect to both scheduling meetings and exploring content areas. Through the self-evaluations and reflections, one YAG member expressed, "I love them (trainings)! Sometimes I wish there was more time for more in-depth conversations and to look at topics concerning us." Given the age range of the YAG members and core ELAYO team members, the demands on each individual's time differ significantly. While some hold traditional workday schedules, others go to school or have internships in addition to working, limiting their time for extracurricular activities and collaboration with ELAYO. In addition, we have seen that the lack of a consistent date/ time for gatherings and trainings contributes to this scheduling challenge. Once data collection began, the travel necessary for field research became a limiting factor for scheduling meetings and maintaining contact with the YAG. Unfortunately, this coincided with an unforeseen change in staffing, contributing to a lack of continuity. Having a few months between meetings required re-establishing the group dynamic. We have noted this challenge and are working towards both creating more time for in-depth discussions during meetings, as well as continuing to engage YAG members and core team members, alike, to create a more structured meeting day and time. Furthermore, staying connected through the use of social media, especially Facebook, has been a key communication tool and lesson learned. In fact, we have found that emails and phone calls are the least effective forms of communication with the YAG members, while a Facebook message or text usually elicits an immediate response.

Figure 5.

When reflecting on the life of ELAYO, we conclude that the largest lesson learned for adult programmers has been the importance of youth voice. We have heard in resounding unison, from the youth, that no one had posed "these questions" to them before. This points to the lack of space in traditional social settings or educational spheres for conversations about sexual and reproductive decision-making and its impact on education among youth, and for deeper reflection upon the structural factors that they deal with on a daily basis. The longing for a platform for these discussions is palpable among youth. The ensuing discussions that arise about social justice are organic, stemming from observations and lived experience. It is noteworthy that, when given the opportunity, youth are eager to amplify their voices, which are filled with incredible insight and curiosity: "When youth have a voice within contexts that affect them, opportunities for positive youth development emerge" (Serido, Borden and Perkins 45).

Below, we include the reflections from one of our YAG members, who helped formulate this paper and who wanted to make sure she could express—in her own words—the major impacts that serving as a YAG member and participating in the ELAYO-related activities had on her personal and educational aspirations.

¡Presente! : A Youth Advisory Group Member Reflects on Lessons Learned

It has been a great opportunity working in the ELAYO project. What this project did was bring people interested in the Latino population together, and use their experiences to help influence a study. This was not as easy as it sounds. What I really enjoyed was that ELAYO first and foremost created a space where everyone felt comfortable. They did this by creating a location where "the door was always open". Their offices, or the main room where we met, were very inviting. You would immediately feel welcomed. They made getting to know us a priority. They were very helpful in creating ice breakers at the beginning of every meeting, not only to help them get to know us, but for us to get to know each other as a group.

The coordinators would also always find time to remind us of the group rules to ensure that we were all aware of the space we are trying to create. This also helped for us to become trusting of one another and know that we were not going to be attacked or judged. Feeling safe and comfortable was very important when we participated in the activities with CLRJ, because we were exposing our thoughts and opinions to the team. It felt great to know that although some did not agree, our beliefs were respected.

I always felt part of the team when they invited me to join the workshops. It gave me an opportunity to become more informed on a subject I had little knowledge about. The information provided during the presentations was relevant to me, because it was about my people, my culture. During those workshops, the coordinators were always open to questions. They understood that for some of us, it was the first time being exposed to information that pertained to our population.

The ELAYO team was inclusive of everyone, no matter what their background is. It did so by having workshops on what questions they should ask when addressing topics such as education, sexuality, and sex education. They also included us in the naming of the project. They took our input in what the name for the study should be. It made us feel like our help and input was needed to keep the project running.

For many of the members, having been a part of the workshops and creating interview questions, really got them interested in working as researchers. This study served as a gateway for youth to want to do research on other social issues that affected them directly. Exposing youth to this type of work had a positive spin.

I went into the project as a Raza studies major at SFSU, wanting to learn more about issues affecting the Latino population. I had heard about the ELAYO project through one of the female members. She told me I would be part of a study that aims to find factors affecting decision making of Latino youth. I thought it'd be great exposure to the sexual reproductive needs of Latinos. What I got was something greater. Through the project I learned how a research project is started, because we were a part of it since the beginning. I also learned what goes into interview questions. I was given the opportunity to conduct interviews myself. This project helped me figure out where I want to go after graduating. I found that I wanted to work more in public policy, especially in policy affecting the Latino community. ELAYO has played a strong role in shaping our minds in breaking barriers and fight for social justice.

Next Steps for the Youth Advisory Group

We are individuals coming together as a community to change perspectives, create assets, and support each other towards success.

—YAG member, describing their purpose as a group

ELAYO recognizes the already-significant contribution the YAG members have put forth in the project. YAG member participation in the first year contributed to the ELAYO name, logo, research tools, and a unique lens inspired by Latino youth voice. The project would be quite different without the Youth Advisory Group. In fact, the YAG members contributed to an incredibly rich conversation that very clearly countered the current deficit-based framework for youth health, demonstrating incredible intelligence, insight, resilience and—above all—a desire to continue making positive contributions to their community. Allowing youth voices to inform academic and policy efforts will ensure that a shift towards an asset-based framework is achieved.

As integral as the YAG has been to the success of this project thus far, the team-in-training model, with the alternative educational pipeline at its core, has been equally influential in the growth and development of the YAG members. Their participation in the research process has allowed them to acquire skills in research methods and has deepened their knowledge within the fields of sexual and reproductive health and rights, Latino populations, and educational equity. Moreover, ELAYO has supported the pursuit of higher education, and fostered career interests in the social science and sexuality realm.

Furthermore, the impact of our alternative educational pipeline has proven influential throughout the course of the project, as evidenced by the trajectory of our YAG members through their academic endeavors. All of our high school YAG members have since graduated from high school and pursued higher education. Two high school YAG members will be attending four-year universities beginning in the fall of 2013, after receiving offers from multiple universities. The remaining high school YAG members will continue their education at a community college, with the hopes of soon transferring to four-year universities.

Consistent with the high-school YAG members' educational trajectory, all of our undergraduate YAG members have since graduated from San Francisco State University with their bachelor's degrees. One of the undergraduate YAG members is pursuing a graduate degree, and has been admitted to a Masters of Public Health Program beginning Fall 2013. The other undergraduate members have entered the workforce to gain experiential knowledge, and they express the desire to pursue a graduate degree in the future.

One of our top priorities for the next phase of ELAYO is to ensure that each team member's individual educational goals are supported. Goal setting and mentoring for each person, regardless of her/his educational path, will lead all of those involved in ELAYO to become more proactive about each person's individual and collective educational aspirations. Together we will continue to access the mentoring resources we have created within ELAYO's team of adults and youth, particularly reaching out to the YAG members transitioning to new educational or work environments, and providing guidance and support.

Closing Remarks

> ...*I am a part of ELAYO because I believe in empowering Latino youth.*
>
> —YAG member

ELAYO: Empower Latino Youth has been an immeasurable opportunity for many of those involved. Honoring youth voice, being part of a collaborative process with California Latinas for Reproductive Justice (CLRJ) and allowing for mentorship to occur through an alternative educational pipeline are some methods that have made ELAYO a unique project. Though the research process is nearly over, the learning process is still in its infancy. As findings from the research emerge, the continued partnership with CLRJ and the YAG continue to inform the interpretation of these findings, along with influencing the discussion around themes and appropriate courses of action through policy advocacy.

Protecting the sexual health and rights of our youth should be a priority for parents, teachers, mentors, and policymakers alike if we are truly invested in the future of our nation. Engaging Latino youth to help develop creative and effective ways to improve policies and programs that impact their own sexual and reproductive health and rights provides a necessary model for transforming social norms, reducing negative discourse, and elevating youth voices. To follow ELAYO: Empower Latino Youth please visit: http://healthequity.sfsu.edu/our-work/research/elayo.html; https://www.facebook.com/elayoproject; https://twitter.com/ElayoProject.

Acknowledgments

A very heartfelt thank you to the Youth Advisory Group members: Abigail Flores, Eva Gonzalez, Heidi Lucas, Brenda Ortiz, Alberto Rodriguez, Alex Serrano, Marisa Tragsiel and Miguel A. Torres. We would also like to thank the Ford Foundation for their generous support of ELAYO.

Endnotes

1. The term Latino will be used in this paper to include persons of Cuban, Mexican, Puerto Rican, South or Central American, or other Spanish culture or origin regardless of race or gender. If we mean to specify by gender, we will still use the English-language adjective Latino for either Latino male or Latino female as opposed to the Spanish-language gender-based nouns of Latino and Latina to avoid confusion of terminology.

Works Cited

Afable-Munsuz, Aimee and Claire D. Brindis. "Acculturation and the Sexual and Reproductive Health of Latino Youth in the United States: A Literature Review." *Perspectives On Sexual and Reproductive Health* 38.4 (2006): 208-19. Print.

Ayón, Cecilia, and Michela Bou Ghosn Naddy. "Latino Immigrant Families' Social Support Networks: Strength and Limitations During a Time of Stringent Immigration Legistlation and Economic Insecurity." *Journal of Community Psychology* 41.3 (2013): 359-77. Print.

California Adolescent Sexual Health Work Group. *2007 Data for California Adolescent Births, AIDS, STDs*, 2009. PDF file.

California Department of Public Health. "CA Teen Birth Rates 2008." Data & Statistics. 2010.

California Latinas for Reproductive Justice. "Young Women Speak Out! Perspectives and Implications of Reproductive Health, Rights and Justice Policies." *CLRJ Research Reports* 2.1 (2010).

Centers for Disease Control and Prevention. "Cases of HIV infection and AIDS in the United States." *HIV/AIDS Surveillance Report* 13.2 (2002): 1-44.

Cox, Mary F. "Racial Differences in Parenting Dimensions and Adolescent Condom Use at Sexual Debut." *Public Health Nursing* 23.1 (2006): 2-10. Print.

Denner, Jill, Douglas Kirby, Karin Coyle and Claire Brindis. "The Protective Role of Social Capital and Cultural Norms in Latino Communities: A Study of Adolescent Births." *Hispanic Journal of Behavioral Sciences* 23.1 (2001): 3-21. Print.

Guilamo-Ramos, Vincent, et al. "The Content and Process of Mother-Adolescent Communication About Sex in Latino Families." *Social Work Research* 30.3 (2006): 169-81. Print.

Israel, Barbara A., et al. "Critical Issues in Developing and Following Community-Based Participatory Research Principles." *Community-Based Participatory Research for Health*. Ed. Meredith Minkler and Nina Wallerstein. San Francisco: Jossey-Bass, 2003. 47-66. Print.

Lerner, Richard M., Jason B. Almerigi, Christina Theokas, and Jacqueline V. Lerner. "Positive Youth Development A View of the Issues." *The Journal of Early Adolescence* 25.1 (2005): 10-16. Print.

Ozer, Emily J., and Laura Douglas. "The Impact of Participatory Research on Urban Teens: An Experimental Evaluation." *American Journal of Community Psychology* 51.1-2 (2013): 66-75. Print.

Powers, Jane L., and Jennifer S. Tiffany. "Engaging Youth in Participatory Research and Evaluation." *Journal of Public Health Management and Practice* November Supplement (2006): S79–S87. Print.

Reyes, Jazmin A., and Maurice J. Elias. "Fostering social-emotional resilience among Latino youth." *Psychology in the Schools* 48.7 (2011): 723- 737. Print.

Rodriguez, Michael C. and Diana Morrobel. "A Review of Latino Youth Development Research and a Call for an Asset Orientation." *Hispanic Journal of Behavioral Sciences* 26.2 (2004): 107-27. Print.

Serido, Joyce, Lynne M. Borden, and Daniel F. Perkins. "Moving Beyond Youth Voice." *Youth & Society* 43.1 (2009): 44-63. Print.

Shor, Ira and Paolo Freire. *A Pedagogy for Liberation: Dialogues on Transforming Education*. Bergin & Garvey Publisher, Inc.: South Hadley MA, 1987. Print.

Elodia Villaseñor, MPH, ELAYO Project Coordinator, Health Equity Institute, San Francisco State University (SFSU) (elodia@sfsu.edu); Miguel Alcalá, ELAYO Research Assistant, Health Equity Instititue, SFSU (Alcala93@mail.sfsu.edu); Ena Suseth Valladares, MPH, Director of Research, California Latinas for Reproductive Justice (Ena.clrj@gmail.com); Miguel A. Torres, ELAYO Youth Advisory Group Member & Interviewer, SFSU (miguelt@ail.sfsu.edu); Vanessa Mercado, MPH, ELAYO Research Associate, Health Equity Institute, SFSU (mercado@mail.sfsu.edu); and Cynthia A. Gómez, PhD, Director & Professor, Health Equity Institute, SFSU (drcgomez@sfsu.edu).

Addressing Economic Devastation and Built Environment Degradation to Prevent Violence: A Photovoice Project of Detroit Youth Passages

Louis F. Graham, Armando Matiz Reyes, William Lopez, Alana Gracey, Rachel C. Snow, Mark B. Padilla

This project increased awareness about issues of violence to youth, their communities, and policy makers through the technique of photovoice and its translation into photo exhibitions and other community events. Youth participants learned photography skills, engaged in critical communal discussions about important issues affecting their health, wrote reflective stories about their photos, and engaged in policy change efforts. Their photos depict the need to address economic devastation and built environment degradation to prevent violence in their communities. Youth presented policy makers and community leaders with an "insider's perspective" of the issues facing their communities, with the hope of promoting policy change.

Detroit Youth Passages (DYP) strives to amplify voices, promote understanding, and create change by working with Latino youth and young African-American cisgender and transgender women (Lopez et al.). Using a praxis-based approach, DYP seeks to examine and positively transform the structural conditions that contribute to sexual vulnerabilities. The project is a partnership between the University of Michigan School of Public Health, the Detroit Hispanic Development Corporation (DHDC), Alternatives For Girls (AFG), and the Ruth Ellis Center (REC). DYP leaders invited young people to participate on the DYP steering committee at the project's inception. Project leadership recognized the importance of a youth-driven space from which young people could help shape the project's direction and lead activities with greater autonomy, outside of the project's steering committee, which is led by researchers. The Youth Advisory Board (YAB) was established in the spring of 2011, and comprised nine representatives between 18-24 years of age from communities served by the Detroit-based partner organizations: DHDC, AFG, and REC (Table 1).

    The partner organizations were engaged as community stakeholders from the beginning of the DYP project. DHDC creates opportunities for Latino youth and their families by providing high-quality, innovative and culturally appropriate programs and services that focus on employment, education, and violence prevention. AFG serves homeless and high-risk girls and young women by providing safe shelter, street outreach, and educational support, among other critical services. REC provides residential and drop-in programs for LGBTQ youth and helps young people find pathways to safety and independence.

    In the summer of 2011, DYP leaders secured funding from the Detroit Community-Academic Urban Research Center's (URC) planning grant initiative to support the DYP Youth Advisory Board. The Detroit URC is a community-based participatory research (CBPR) partnership that conducts interventions to reduce and ultimately eliminate health inequities. The YAB provided its members with the resources they needed to identify challenges and assets in their communities. Using a consensus-based approach, the YAB settled on violence as a core issue facing many youth communities in Detroit.

Table 1: Youth Advisory Board Demographics

Demographics	N
Ethnicity	
African-American	6
Latino	3
Gender	
Cis-Men	2
Cis-Women	4
Trans-Women	3
Education	
Currently in HS	6
Not currently in HS and not completed	1
GED	2
Average Age	19

This article focuses on a youth-driven photovoice project that contributes to public discourse on causes and prevention of violence across communities positioned differently vis-à-vis race, ethnicity, gender, sexuality, and sexual vulnerability: young Latino men and women, and African-American cisgender and transgender women. Photography served as a medium to both amplify youth voices and to gather research data on structural factors that influence experiences of violence. This photovoice project sought to address violence and its possible solutions in Detroit youth communities. It further intended to generate dialogue and action among youth, community leaders, and policy makers toward violence prevention.

Detroit Context

In part due to the collapse of the auto industry and foreclosure crises, Detroit had—at the height of the recent economic recession (2009)—the highest unemployment rate of any urban center in the nation (Bureau of Labor Statistics). Homelessness was unrivaled by other US cities, with a rate of 216 per 10,000 residents (Homelessness Research Institute)—nearly twice as high as the second-ranking urban area in the United States. HIV rates among African-American and Latino youth were also high and growing rapidly (Michigan Department of Community Health). Nevertheless, the resolve of Detroit communities was strong, as evident in the work and successes of our partner organizations.

The negative impacts of these structural conditions were greatest among youth. In 2009, 31% of Detroit Public School students reported being in a physical fight, 20% missed school because they did not feel safe, and 9% carried a weapon (Bing 3). The homicide rate among youth aged 15-24 was 80.5 deaths per 100,000, a rate more than five times the rate outside of Wayne County, within which Detroit is located (Bing 3). Also, one in five women in Michigan with current partners was the victim of physical violence in that relationship according to a representative survey (Healthy Michigan). The average age of photovoice participants was 19 years old, the majority of the group was currently completing high school, and YAB members included Black and Latino men and cis- and transgender women.

Detroit is a microcosm of national violence trends for underserved Black and Latino communities in urban centers. For example, in 2009, homicide was one of the ten leading causes of death for both Blacks and Latinos, with 19.9 and 6.6 homicides per 100,000 population, respectively (Heron 7). For Latino men ages 20-24, the approximate age range of YAB members, the homicide rate climbed to 28.4 per 100,000. While there are no sample statistics that can accurately estimate population parameters, the little data that exists estimates the number of hate crimes perpetrated against transgender individuals to be 213 per year over a ten-year period (Stotzer 170-179).

These marginalized populations further face challenges due to diminished social networks resulting from incarceration, immigration status, or tensions related to gender transition practices. To address these articulating economic and health contexts, DYP focused on the relationships between residential instability, joblessness, and situations or environments that undermine healthy sexual identity development and sexual health. The YAB began to link structural factors to everyday violence. That youth would want to both elucidate and address the effects of this violence in their lives was not surprising, and photovoice could provide a means to do so.

Method

As word spread about DYP through the partner organizations, staff recruited interested youth to serve on the YAB. The YAB description and announcement solicited individuals committed to issues of social justice for young people in Detroit who were responsible enough to follow through on commitments and able to dedicate approximately five hours per week to the project. Youth who chose to participate received: $100 per month; an opportunity to share with their friends and communities research findings from the DYP project gathered during the summer; and training in research, recruitment, and communication strategies. Consistent with the principles of CBPR, the YAB was encouraged by DYP leadership to structure its own rules and regulations regarding participation.

Ultimately, members were expected to attend regularly scheduled meetings and trainings for project activities; provide feedback to the larger DYP team on research findings; and practice community leadership skills by sharing their experiences and knowledge with other youth in their communities.[1] Participants used a co-chair and subcommittee organizational structure for the YAB and developed their own agreements (Table 2). After much discussion, they decided that although their respective communities were affected by different kinds of violence such as sexual, transphobic, and gang violence, violence itself was endemic. The YAB was interested in actively addressing violence, not simply learning about it. DYP leadership suggested photovoice as a research method, since it extends beyond data collection and analysis, to effect intentional, policy-relevant action.

Table 2: Youth Advisory Board Rules and Regulations as created by team members

- Keep an open mind—I will be meeting and working with a diverse group of young people from around Detroit. It is important that I treat everyone with respect.
- Participate—I understand that there are approximately eight hours a month of activities and meetings for the project.
- Be Consistent—I understand that regular attendance at meetings and trainings is necessary for project activities to run smoothly.

Photovoice

Photovoice is a participatory research method that blends a grassroots approach to photography with social action (Wang 185-192). It involves participants taking photos, telling stories, and building their capacity to act as catalysts for social change in their communities. This research method is a participatory means of sharing experiences and influencing public policy through the immediacy of visual images and their accompanying narratives. Photovoice has three main goals: 1) to enable people to record and reflect their community's strengths and concerns; 2) to promote critical dialogue and knowledge about personal and community issues through large- and small-group discussion of photographs; and 3) to reach policy makers (Wang).

Photovoice has been used successfully by researchers, health departments, and community organizations to assess the needs of communities while eliciting the self-described concerns of those communities (Duffy), including young people living in Detroit (Schultz et al.). This method acknowledges community members as empowered critical thinkers and problem solvers—assets to their communities. The current study was approved by the University of Michigan's Health and Behavioral Sciences Institutional Review Board. Inclusion criteria included the following: Detroit metropolitan area residents between the ages of 18 and 24 years old, who self-identified as either: Latino/a or African-American woman (cisgender, transgender, or other designation).

Data Collection and Analysis

Over three half-days, DYP project leadership trained youth in, (1) the ethics and safety considerations of photographing in their communities, (2) photography techniques, and (3) Holga camera use. This training included instructions on avoiding the documentation of identifiable faces and illicit activity, such as gang activity. Participants brainstormed potential risk situations and effective ways of dealing with them. Locations deemed unsafe were added to a list of prohibited areas. DYP leaders offered location alternatives that were similar enough to convey the intended visual message while keeping YAB members safe. If a participant wanted to take a photo of a house known for its illicit drug activity, for instance, s/he collaborated with project leadership to find a similar house in a safer situation. In their storytelling and discussion about the photo, youth could mention that this house was not a drug house, but looked very similar to another where they felt unsafe photographing.

Youth were encouraged to be creative, to photograph in groups, and to carry the list of prohibited places and activities with them when taking photos. For the same safety concerns, youth were discouraged from taking photos at night. Youth first signed a consent form according to protocol. Cameras with black-and-white film were distributed to YAB members, who were asked to take ten photos over the course of one week that captured causes of violence in their communities.

Film cameras were used to: 1) offer youth the option of double exposure shots (i.e., using same segment of film to capture multiple images that overlay), 2) improve youth photography skills by encouraging them to focus on the camera and setting to capture a good shot initially, rather than relying on the trial-and-error technique used with digital cameras (i.e., view image immediately, and if not to liking, delete and shoot again), and 3) discourage sharing or downloading images (e.g., share through social media), which was prohibited. The following week, DYP staff developed the film and destroyed or modified (e.g., blurred faces) any implicating photos before they were shown to the YAB as a group. The photos were then returned to their owners, who had an opportunity to take additional photos during the next week, if they were not satisfied with their first shoot. During the final week, participants met at the Detroit Hispanic Development Corporation for two to three hours to discuss their photos.

DYP project leaders led YAB youth in the SHOWeD analysis (Table 3), which entailed critical reflection, dialogue, writing, and narrative-sharing (Wallerstein and Sanchez-Merki). In this study, each member of the YAB was asked to select two photos to share for group discussion. Through answering the SHOWeD questions and combining their photos with text, youth and project leadership began to delineate themes, and to theorize the relationships between these themes. During the course

Table 3: SHOWeD Analysis

1. What did you See happening here?
2. What is really Happening?
3. How does this relate to Our lives?
4. Why does this problem/condition/asset exist?
5. What can we Do about it?

of this discussion, if youth felt that any of their other eight photos were similar to, or resonated with, any of the other YAB member photos discussed, they could introduce the photo to be included in the discussion.

Youth then selected 10 of the 18 photos for which to summarize their collective response to each question. The group abstracted themes from across response summaries. Photos representing similar themes were grouped for presentation. This process was repeated using color film to take photos that youth believed captured how violence is prevented or successfully addressed in their communities. Black and white film was used: 1) prior to the use of color film because of black and white film's versatility (i.e., suits almost any type of photography and adapts well to all lighting situations) since youth were still learning and becoming familiar with photography; and 2) to help create contrast between photos that represented causes of violence and those representing ways of addressing violence, which were captured on color film.

Color film was used to capture ways of addressing violence to capitalize on its attention-grabbing and connotative qualities and range. The YAB wanted these photos to elicit feelings of hopefulness, possibility, and a vibrant Detroit. DYP leaders took detailed notes throughout each discussion session with YAB members, focusing on non-verbal information, over-talk dialogue, and descriptions of how photo names and captions were developed. Finally, youth wrote captions and titles for the twenty selected photos: ten black-and-white photos representing causes of violence, and ten color photos representing ways to address violence.

Findings: Causes of Violence

YAB youth had been prompted to "take photos that capture causes of violence in your community." From these photos and the accompanying discussion of SHOWeD questions, two themes emerged: Youth believed that, 1) Economic desperation silences communities, destroys families (e.g., through divorce and decreased social support), and contributes to gang and drug activity; and, 2) Abandoned and forgotten spaces are conducive to serving as sites of violence, including rape and murder.

Economic Desperation

Photos of money, graffiti, and cars that represented drug sales, apprehension by police while stealing, and entertainment constituted one set of the black-and-white photographs. The youth photographers discussed how families lack income to survive,

Figure 1. Money in the shadows.

and how this financial lack causes neighborhood problems like violence and a heavy police presence. These conditions make it more difficult to earn money, as businesses leave and property values fall—a never ending cycle of "needing money to make money." The economic desperation felt by some in these communities drove them to robberies, theft, and gang violence related to the drug economy. Financial strain contributed to relationship challenges within families, which were in turn related to parental divorce and residential instability among young people.

Youth focused on how drugs are perceived by some as an escape from problems related to economic insecurity, and how gang members and other youth "tag" (make graffiti) to mark symbolic territory because they have little to call their own, and because they feel silenced. This silencing sometimes leads them to "lash out." Young people create graffiti art as a way of indicating symbolic ownership of their neighborhood. The cycle of poverty, drug use, and violence was found earlier in interviews conducted with young people of similar age and demographics in Detroit (Lopez et al.).

Participants felt that the images could educate their communities by communicating that people do not prefer to buy and sell drugs, yet they need more income; and by getting people to understand the generational elements of violence related to poverty. Lastly, youth conveyed that higher paying jobs, more businesses, and a greater city-wide policy and programmatic focus on youth could help remediate economic desperation and associated violence.

Abandoned Spaces

The second set of black-and-white photos principally featured deserted fields, lots, and buildings, capturing the widespread loss of homes and businesses in Detroit. YAB members dialogued about how rundown spaces are areas where violence may

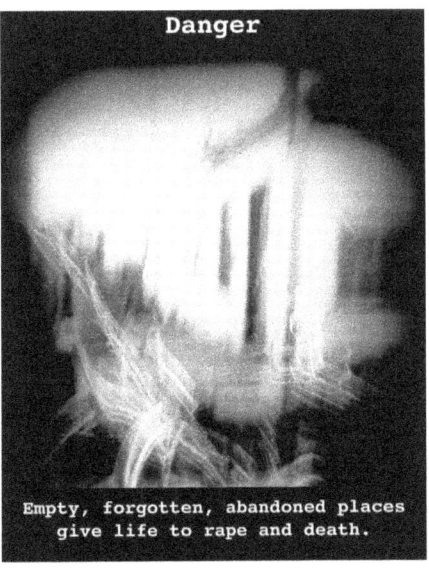

Figure 2. Danger. *Figure 3. A lost road.*

concentrate, and where murders and rapes more easily occurred and yet are some of the few places children have to play. They concluded that abandoned spaces remain abandoned because no one takes responsibility for them, and city-wide injustices—like governmental corruption—hamstring redevelopment. Youth thought their photographic images could educate policy-makers about the need to clean up, rebuild, and invest in underdeveloped neighborhoods.

Findings: Violence Prevention

After documenting causes of violence, youth were prompted to "take photos that capture how violence is prevented or successfully addressed in your community." Two themes from the photos on prevention (or, how violence has been successfully addressed in some instances) emerged: 1) local institutions providing resources and services to help alleviate economic devastation and support economically depressed communities help preempt violence, and 2) a focus on youth education, recreation, and neighborhood development creates economic opportunities for youth and addresses built environment degradation.

Resources and Services

The first set of color photos featured organizations and centers such as museums, churches, and drug abuse recovery agencies that offer facilities, assistance, and jobs to marginalized communities. Conversations around the photos concentrated on how such agencies help in the areas of health, income, and childcare, alleviating the economic devastation that contributes to violence. Youth thought these community organizations arose from the commitment and dedication of their leadership, and suggested that their images illustrated how funding and motivation can stabilize neighborhoods by addressing inequities and violence. Lastly, they indicated that there should be efforts to leverage, enhance, and expand community assets by increasing decision-making diversity and better promoting community resources and services, particularly by celebrating those who have stayed in Detroit and are creating opportunities for others.

Figure 4. Helping hand.

Education, Recreation, and Development

The second set of color photos featured schools, musical instruments, and playgrounds, symbolizing learning, culture, and fun. Youth reflected on how they feel empowered when they learn about their history and are able to exercise their creativity through art. They felt that if more youth had such opportunities, those youth would be less inclined toward violence, and would learn nonviolent forms of resistance to oppression. Participants decided that their assets, such as education, culture, and empowerment, are rooted in their talents, luck, and the kindness and love of teachers, family, and community, the beginning of what it will take to address community violence. The youth hoped that their communities could capitalize on their visual representation of community assets by increasing the number of safe spaces for young artists to gather and perform, by supporting entrepreneurship programs, and by showing pride in the city. Entrepreneurship opportunities could mitigate the economic desperation that contributes to violence, and showing more pride in the city could help decrease the number of abandoned spaces available for violence to occur.

Figure 5. Speaking with music.

Figure 6. Nothing will stop us.

Mobilizing Community Awareness and Policy Change

The YAB organized community exhibitions of their photos and stories. The first gallery exhibition took place in June of 2012 at the Ford Foundation's convening for grantees of the Youth, Sexuality, Health, and Rights initiative. Held at the University of Michigan, Detroit Center, DYP leadership introduced the project and YAB members circulated throughout the gallery, adding their stories and answering questions from university scholars, community partners, students, and youth from across the country. Invitees to the gallery were moved by the experience. The YAB was enthusiastic about presenting at the convening because they wanted to paint a picture of Detroit, as seen through their eyes, for those from outside of Michigan. All those involved in the DYP project thought there may be synergistic experiences between youth in Detroit and youth working with the other Ford-funded projects that could form the basis of future collaborations.

The YAB also organized a violence prevention forum, UProar (Urging Peace through Resilience, Opportunity, Action and Restoration), in which photos were exhibited to funders, local policy makers, community leaders, representatives from community-based organizations, and other youth. Through UProar, which took place on June 21, 2012, the YAB sought to raise awareness, further dialogue, and strategize solutions to youth violence in Detroit. UProar took place at Alternatives For Girls (AFG) where Detroit Mayor Dave Bing's Violence Prevention Initiative representatives, the Youth Violence Prevention Taskforce Co-chair, City Councilman James Tate, and Dr. Kofi Adoma of the Ruth Ellis Center all gave keynote addresses. Speakers told personal stories of how violence had impacted their lives, talked about past and current prevention efforts, and encouraged youth to get more involved. They also fielded challenging questions from youth about how city government works, governmental transparency, and acting on youth ideas for violence prevention.

The event featured a domestic violence discussion lead by YAB members, a gang violence workshop led by AFG staff, and an Urban Arts Academy training led by Detroit Hispanic Development Corporation (DHDC) staff. UProar also featured youth performers from DHDC and Ruth Ellis Center, a screening of the documentary, Interrupters, and the presence of a number of community-based organizations and programs. All youth in attendance took a youth violence prevention pledge. Around fifty people attended; 35% percent of attendees had been the victim of violence, and 25% had at some point perpetrated violence against others. The YAB participated in several further events showcasing their photos.

Conclusion

A community-based participatory approach using visual methods enabled youth to contribute to the production of knowledge about ways to address sexual, domestic, gang, and other acts of violence. This project aimed to contribute to improved social and health-related climates for youth by providing evidence of the ways that environments contribute to vulnerabilities using aesthetic forms of knowledge dissemination to generate dialogue on how policy-makers and stakeholders might work together to improve conditions and maximize resilience (Meyer; Graham) for youth. The project helped to build community capacity by empowering youth to creatively express what they felt were the most important issues in their communities. It is the authors' hope that the project might assist other youth groups who want to undertake a similar project, particularly those who seek to extend the use of photovoice to understudied and underserved populations, by providing useful information and evidence of success.

Acknowledgments

Youth Advisory Board—Casandra T., Krystina Edwards, Eddi Gonzales, Kymberli R., Lakyra Dawson, Tamisha Johnson, Ramon Mendez, Asha D., Ashley A., and Ashia

Davis; UM Team—Jessica Moorman and Raelle Saulson; Community Co-Investigators—Laura A Hughes, Angela Reyes, and Deena Policicchio; and the Detroit Urban Research Center.

Endnotes

1. Most YAB members adhered to the membership agreements for the majority of the project period. At times, some members had difficulty with transportation and managing time commitments, causing them to miss some meetings or be delayed in completing an assigned task. YAB members and DYP staff worked to support young people with rides, when needed, and the honorariums appeared sufficient to assist members with other expenses they may have incurred in participation. All participants completed the project.

Works Cited

Bing, Dave. "Youth Violence Prevention Initiative".City of Detroit, 2011. PDF file.

Bureau of Labor Statistics. "Metropolitan Area Employment and Unemployment." 2010. PDF file.

Duffy, Lynne. "Hidden heroines: Lone mothers assessing community health using photovoice." *Health Promotion Practice* 11 (2010): 788-797. Print.

Graham, Louis F. "Psychosocial health of black sexually marginalized men." *Social Determinants of Health among African American Men*. Ed. H.M. Treadwell, C. Xanthos and K.B Holden. San Francisco: Wiley & Sons, 2012. Print.

Healthy Michigan 2010. "Michigan's Surgeon General's Health Status Report." 2010. PDF file.

Heron, Melanie. "Deaths: Leading causes for 2009." *National Vital Statistics Reports* 61 (2012): 7. Print.

Homelessness Research Institute. "Geography of Homelessness, Part 2: Prevalence of Homelessness." 2010. Web. 11 July 2013.

Lopez, William, Louis F. Graham, Caitlin Reardon, Armando Matiz Reyes, Angela Reyes, and Mark Padilla. "'No jobs, more crime. More jobs, less crime': structural factors affecting the health of Latino men in Detroit." *Journal of Men's Health* 9.4 (2012): 255-260. Print.

Meyer, Ilan H. "Identity, stress, and resilience in lesbians, gay men, and bisexuals of color." *Counseling Psychologist* 38.3 (2010): 442-454. Print.

Michigan Department of Community Health. "Quarterly HIV/AIDS Report, Michigan." 2010. Web. 11 July 2013.

Schulz, Amy J., Barbara A. Israel, Chris M. Coombe, Causandra Gaines, Angela G. Reyes, Zachary Rowe, Sharon L. Sand, Larkin L. Strong, and Sheryl Weir. "A community-based participatory planning process and multilevel intervention design: toward eliminating cardiovascular health inequities." *Health Promotion Practice* 12.6 (2011): 900-911. Print.

Stotzer, Rebecca. "Violence against transgender people: A review of United States data." *Aggression and Violent Behavior* 14.3 (2009): 170-179. Print.

Wang, Caroline. "Photovoice: A participatory action research strategy applied to women's health." *Journal of Women's Health* 8.2 (1999): 185-192. Print.

Wallerstein, Nina, and Victoria Sanchez-Merki. "Freirian praxis in health education: research results from an adolescent prevention program." *Health Education Research* 9.1 (1994): 105-118. Print.

Louis F. Graham, DrPH, MPH, Assistant Professor, Department of Public Health, University of Massachusetts–Amherst (LFGraham@schoolph.umass.edu); Armando Matiz Reyes, DDS, Research Area Specialist, Department of Health Behavior and Health Education, University of Michigan School of Public Health (armandom@umich.edu); William Lopez, MPH, Graduate Research Assistant, Department of Health Behavior and Health Education, University of Michigan School of Public Health (wlopez1982@gmail.com); Alana Gracey, Street Outreach Manager, Outreach & Education Services, Alternatives For Girls, Detroit, Michigan (agracey@alternativesforgirls.org.); Rachel C. Snow, ScD, Associate Professor, Department of Health Behavior and Health Education, University of Michigan School of Public Health (rsnow@unfpa.org); Mark B. Padilla, PhD, MPH, Associate Professor, Global and Sociocultural Studies, School of International and Public Affairs, Florida International University (marpadi@fiu.edu).

Paying to Listen: Notes from a Survey of Sexual Commerce

Rachel C. Snow, Angela Williams, Curtis Collins, Jessica Moorman, Tomas Rangel, Audrey Barick, Crystal Clay, Armando Matiz Reyes

As the study of sexual commerce has grown dramatically in recent decades due to interest in HIV/AIDS, an expanded literature has scrutinized how research teams manage the operational challenges of accessing spaces that typically resist scrutiny. This paper ventures a combination of both scholarly reflections on the utility of ethical listening and specific methodologies for working with hard-to-reach populations, and selective use of field notes to illustrate the ethical and operational challenges of data collection with marginalized youth. The paper highlights several pivotal commitments and procedures for generating an effective community-based research project, the extent of time demanded for such research, and collective reflections on the potential for both harm and good in such projects. Efforts to understand the social context in which young adults engage in sexual exchange—both on the street and in erotic dance clubs—requires a commitment to ethical listening, and to progressive learning.

Background: Detroit Youth Passages (DYP)

The survey described in these notes is part of a larger project designed to explore the structural factors affecting the sexual health and well-being of Detroit youth. The Detroit Youth Passages (DYP) study is a four-year, mixed-methods project that utilizes a human rights framework, and uses research to design and develop new interventions for empowering communities of young people in Detroit. The primary methods of the study have been described elsewhere (Lopez et al.), but included more than 300 hours of participant observation; 60 semi-structured interviews; more than 30 life histories with residentially unstable youth and former sex workers; and a survey of 278 young people working in a variety of venues for sexual commerce, including street-based sex work and erotic and lap dancing in strip clubs. The project leverages a partnership between the University of Michigan and three community-based organizations (CBOs) in Detroit that provide social services to residentially unstable youth: the Detroit Hispanic Development Corporation (DHDC), which serves Latino/as at risk of gang violence; Alternatives for Girls (AFG), which serves young women engaged in erotic dancing and commercial sex; and the Ruth Ellis Center (REC), which serves homeless lesbian, gay, bisexual and trans youth.

The venue-based survey described in this paper built on more than a year of ethnographic study, including outreach volunteering with community partner agencies, six months of planning with a community-academic research team, and three months of preliminary work conducting informal discussions with dancers and managers in clubs offering various combinations of erotic dancing, lap dancing, and prostitution. The study also included data-gathering in clubs not offering any explicit forms of sexual commerce. While other segments of the overall project include the design of new interventions and outreach, the goal for this segment of the project was explicitly research-focused, aiming for between 200-300 on-site interviews with young people over six to eight weeks.

This manuscript, in content and overall design, aims to elaborate the "progressive learning" of the overall study team, illustrating the essential nature of long-term partnering (in this case, over four years), which we believe should both precede and follow such a survey effort. Such situated engagement facilitates access to spaces that are routinely protected and off-limits to scholarly scrutiny. Building on a growing scholarship concerning how to address the ethical and methodological challenges of research with marginalized, hard-to-access persons (Couch, Durant and Hill; Elias et al.; Holloway and Jefferson; Remple et al.; Shaver; Wahab; Wietzer), we reflect on challenges of otherness and access, debates over compensation, the risks of doing harm, the potential for good, and the cultivation of equality through ethical listening. Grounded in feminist research commitments to make the social position of the researcher visible and encourage those engaged in research to reflect on their own experiences (Harding), we include field notes and quotes from a selection of team members. By including these documented reflections, we attempt to "flip the lens" and examine the project from the experience of project members, highlighting some of the emotional and ethical challenges encountered by project members who bridge the often disparate domains of community, academia, and activism.

Progressive Learning[1]: Long-term Partnerships and Ethnographic Research

Five members of the survey research team had spent much of the preceding 18 months conducting ethnographic research in many of the venues that were planned for this survey. The goal of the ethnography was to explore and document the social and structural conditions of residentially unstable youth, and the implications of those circumstances for their sexual health and well-being. Ethnography was facilitated through the guidance of CBO staff liaisons, and included more than 300 hours of participant observation (with extensive development of shared field notes), 60 semi-structured interviews and 30 life histories with residentially unstable youth and adults associated with the partner agencies.

Much of the ethnographic research highlighted the economic stress that youth were facing in circumstances of chronic under-employment, weak education systems, fragile families, and limited public services. Interviews also highlighted the extent to which residentially unstable youth were coping economically through various forms of sexual commerce, but with quite distinct experiences of distress and violence depending on the venues where they worked: these included the street, strip clubs, and more expensive erotic dancing clubs. We therefore included participant observation in youths' employment spaces such as strip clubs and bars, recruiting youth for in-depth interviews from these spaces, as well as from street-based sex work. Contact with street-based sex workers was made possible because DYP team members were volunteering for weekly nighttime street outreach to sex workers, a service carried out by one of our partner CBOs for more than a decade. Through these outreach activities, our team members gained familiarity with the locales and schedules of street-based sexual commerce, and became acquainted with individual sex workers.

The ethnography, therefore, posed a range of questions regarding how youth become located in one space or another for sexual commerce, and the extent to which work in these different venues is associated with greater or lesser mental distress and exposure to violence—all questions we decided to explore in a follow-up survey. The ethnographic protocols, their primary findings, and the protocol for the follow-up survey were each designed by a Project Steering Committee that included two directors; one outreach director; three staff liaisons from the partner CBOs; four senior researchers; and research staff that included more than six graduate students.

The difficulties of gathering valid data among research participants engaged in illegal activities such as sex work have been extensively addressed (Remple et al., Weitzer, Hubbard, Flowers, Bolton). Most of this literature underscores the challenges of securing access to, and establishing trust and rapport with, such populations. These challenges affect, in turn, the validity of responses. Sex work is generally not available for observation, and therefore demands an exceptionally sensitive appreciation for the complexity of the "field site," which remains partly obscured.[2] Indeed, these challenges have been addressed by some researchers by temporarily inhabiting the work life they seek to study—i.e. becoming strippers (Seymour) or phone sex providers (Flowers). An alternative approach is to recruit sex workers in health or service settings (Dalla et al., Dalla); through existing outreach services that already make routine visits to brothels, strip clubs, or workers on the street; or in designated "safe houses" for counseling, prevention or drug support (Jeal and Salisbury, Wahab).

Our goal was to explore the structural life circumstances that shaped the exchange of sex for resources among Detroit youth, and to compare these conditions across a range of different venues within which sex was exchanged. We were recruiting a comparatively young population of respondents, and wanted to avoid over-selection of clients already connected (directly or indirectly) to the CBOs who were our central partners in the overall four-year project. The CBOs were also keen to better understand the needs of youth who *were not* availing themselves of CBO services, adding to our shared motivation to recruit outside the network of peer contacts who staff the CBOs. We were also wary of the selection bias that could result from either recruitment in service settings or the use of intermediaries with established contact networks. The DYP ethnography of the prior year had highlighted the extent to which many youth in these settings emphasized their social isolation and articulated a climate of distrust among sex workers, leaving us concerned that respondent driven sampling (RDS) would lead us into select, closed networks (for which it was designed). We feared that this would work against our intention to access and compare the life conditions of youth across different sexual commerce venues. Thus, while we initially considered RDS, for the above reasons we ultimately chose a venue-based survey with direct, face-to-face recruitment. Direct contact recruitment was possible because of the preceding ethnographic work (including volunteer work) that had been carried out by a core of the survey team members and who had by now established rapport with managers, dancers, and individuals engaged in sex work on the street.

Team Composition
The survey team included 11 members in total. Five members from the ethnographic research team were joined by two staff recommended from our partner CBOs, two community members, one new DYP project staff member from Detroit with extensive field outreach in the community, and one local graduate student who was already a volunteer at one of our CBOs. Most team members bridged more than one category of academic researcher, activist, or community member, blurring distinctions in ways that facilitated team-building. For example, all but one member had worked or volunteered with at least one of the partner CBOs prior to the survey, and many of the researchers had a history of direct activist work in similar communities. A majority lived in, or were from, Detroit, and community members were themselves graduate students at other universities. The three senior research staff had more than 40 years of field research between them, most with marginalized populations, including male and female sex workers, and long histories of activist work.

Preliminary Work
While many of the team members had gained familiarity with the proposed recruitment sites for the survey, we had not attempted to conduct interviews in these locations, where lights were low, music was loud, alcohol and weed were in use, and lap dancing was underway. Once the team was established, therefore, we spent almost ten weeks before administering the survey conducting preliminary visits to potential recruitment locations (clubs and the street). The primary purpose of these preliminary visits was talking with club managers about potential recruitment, learning when shift changes occurred, getting familiar with bartenders and bouncers, discussing our plans with youth in the business, and gradually learning the times when dancers or street youth might be less encumbered by clients. In several cases, managers recommended preferred hours, but some also told us not to bother coming to their club for research.

Preliminary visits were carried out in teams of two or three members, and guided by weekly team meetings that also served secondary goals, such as internally piloting and refining the survey instrument. The extended preliminary research period also provided an opportunity for the team to discuss the ethics of compensation, methods for creating equality with participants, methods of active and ethical listening, and rapport-building within the team itself. The newer team members amongst us also had time to gradually gain their footing within the project and to enrich our collective knowledge with new perspectives on the proposed venues. The new members also heightened our ambitions for the survey, and were among our strongest advocates for the value of this survey research *for youth themselves.*

Rickard describes a circumstance in which community members with close social access to sex workers became the strongest advocates for conducting formal research on sex work. In the course of conducting AIDS-related research in a London community, Rickard found that it was sex workers and the maids with whom she was living who were most enthusiastic about the prospect of having the personal stories of women who sold sex recorded and shared: "[Prospective participants]… marveled at how wonderful it might be if people in the future could understand history from the actual words and phrases of women who lived the life" (355). Team members with longstanding experience in both research *and* activism in similar communities are often most able to recognize the potential for empowerment through participation, and ensure that such a spirit is effectively included in recruitment language, with phrasing such as: "you are powerful in telling your story, in bearing witness to your own life"; "only you know what this lifestyle is really like, and only you can tell the true story"; "others imagine, but only you really know, so your story is valuable." This sentiment prevailed in our preliminary work, and the recruitment text gained a tone of invitation, participatory ownership and empowerment.

Such empowering language was valuable not only among potential survey participants, but was instrumental in preparing team members for what Beard calls "ethical listening." Elaborating an approach to listening that extends beyond a sociocognitive model of "skills and schemas" deployed to understand messages, Beard argues that "ethical listening" recognizes that good listening is utterly receptive, non-judgmental, silent, and bodily still, and in so being frees the speaker to establish her/his own subjective presence for the listener. Beard highlights the choices we all make in listening, including choices to listen selectively (i.e. for only the precise answers to questioned asked, rather than the fullness of responses) or to not listen, versus listening together, and at best, truly listening to one another. Ethical listening is a prerequisite for progressive learning, and for community-based research that seeks to bridge social marginalization and promote justice.

Three DYP survey research team members—one who had "worked the scene" (participated/ worked in sex work in these same spaces at an earlier phase of life) himself for several years, another who routinely styled hair for erotic dancers, and one acquainted with local sex workers from previous ethnography—discussed the intended research protocol with dancers, sex workers and young people working on the street. Consistent with principles of Community-Based Participatory Research (Israel, Lantz) and Participatory Rural Appraisal (Berardi), those conversations with youth most embedded in the community further sharpened our eventual choice of language and sequence in the survey instrument, as well as plans for recruitment. Creating space for embedded community experts to refine the local adaptation of a protocol is an approach characterizing several of the most in-depth studies among sex workers (Rickard, Wahab).

Validity

Referring to Kinsey's pioneering mid-century sexual behavior surveys, which concluded that people tend to lie about sexual matters, and in unpredictable ways, Elias et al. argue that validity must always be in question in survey research on sex. They predict, "if the researcher encounters problems with gathering [sex] data from the ordinary person, the difficulties with sex workers are much greater." We found this to be not necessarily so. An early conclusion of our team, derived from the first year of ethnographic work, was that for many people engaged in sexual commerce, sex has become *mundane*—not important enough to lie about. Overall, respondents were graphic but matter-of-fact in describing sex and the sexual transactions they offered, and there were few of the behavioral cues identified with intentional misreporting, such as hesitation, skipping questions, vague answers or laughter. These initial observations were borne out early in the survey's pilot-test: those with active engagement with sexual commerce—particularly those selling on the street—were pragmatic and detailed in discussing sexual details. Sex workers did display signs of distress and trauma during interviews, but not in discussing the bodily details of sexual exchange; rather, in response to a range of issues that included childhood experience of trauma, loss of children or parental death, despair over addiction, current crises over a place to stay, and recent exposure to violent clients. The survey team had clear IRB-approved procedural protocols for handling such cases, including use of professional referrals.

Generalizations about what constitutes a "sensitive question" in public health surveys (Groves et al.), hence, may require adjustment when working with sex workers, for whom standard sensitivities about sexual behavior may not apply—at least not when their work is acknowledged *a priori* (by the recruitment setting itself, or by the screening questions). At the same time, other common "sensitive questions" may indeed be universally sensitive, such as questions about early or recent trauma, loss, violence, or even topics such as earnings or income—issues routinely regarded as challenging for survey researchers (Groves et al.). While a majority of our participants were willing to talk about the prices they charged for different sexual acts, there was considerably more avoidance, or vague responses, when reporting the total earnings per night, or earnings per week. There were also numerous cases of possibly inflated responses on total earnings relative to our estimations based on the reported price per act and number of acts per night.

Gaining Access: Working with Managers, Owners, and Gatekeepers

Accessing strip clubs or after-hours clubs is especially challenging when a combination of illegal activities (sex, drugs, possibly underage or undocumented dancers) encourage heightened vigilance on the part of bouncers and managers. When the team was without a male team member on a recruitment outing, we were sometimes unable to enter high-end clubs. The formal or informal rule of many "gentlemen's clubs" is that women are only admitted if they are accompanied by a man. But managers were occasionally suspicious even with men along, while in other clubs—high-end or low—our teams were welcomed without hesitation. With time, we grew better able to predict to which clubs we would gain access—but not without numerous frustrated outings. The following two field note excerpts illustrate our range of experience gaining entry:

> August 4th 2012: Inside [club] our team member and the woman floor manager from last summer meet like friends. Her name is M, and she remembers us from last summer's ethnographic visits—and she's hugging [team member] and me, and making me feel she is so glad we came back. Her warmth is deep and heartfelt.

> August 19th, 2012: We start at [club], but they aren't ready to open, so we sit around outside in deck chairs with a host of feral cats. The dancers are dropped off or brought in by their boyfriends. The group is tight and easy with one another, but we mis-time our discussion. By the time the

bouncer wants to chat with me they've grown suspicious of us, and he says no—"the manager isn't around tonight and I can't agree to this on my own."

While in most clubs we gained initial entry through discussions with owners and managers, it was dancers who frequently helped us to expand our recruitment by serving as ambassadors to other dancers, and sometimes to the club management. Dancers provided us with tips about other clubs, the best times to recruit girls leaving the club, and ideas for getting "in the door" of other locations. On an outing mid-way through data collection, we realized that we could now "read" a club's potential for research within about five minutes—we simply knew the formula. In the field notes below, one can discern our progressive learning about strip club accessibility at the height of data collection:

> August 19th: [The two bouncers] ... are bored because the space feels so empty and they have lots of girls working. The customers are loosely scattered at the bar—there's almost no one at tables. This is good for us. The bouncers agree we can go back to the dressing room and run interviews, so we sit back there and churn out 11 interviews. We know the formula by now—it's quasi empty clubs that work best—slow on business, too many girls for the clientele.

Compensation: Inducement or Respect?

Payment to research subjects raises inevitable ethical concerns over subject agency and possible coercion (Couch et al., Holloway and Jefferson, Martinez-Ebers), especially among subjects who may be extremely poor—as was the case for many of our young participants. We regarded payment as a critical means of recognizing the value of their time. For those who are economically marginalized, payment can offer economic empowerment, and it can establish the message that there is value in sharing their experience as a contribution to public knowledge (Couch et al., Liamputtong). Indeed, many of the participants wanted detailed elaboration about the research objectives, the team, the CBO partners with whom we were working, and our own roles and hopes for the project. Some may have agreed to participate without payment, but Holloway and Jefferson suggest that payment for participation time is also a means of "equalizing the relationship," and is thereby crucial to the balance of power within the partnership of a research interview.

Research participation time also has the potential to compromise earnings for the worker, as the time spent with a researcher may compromise time spent with clients, and therefore can be construed as "taking from" subjects (see Liamputtong 25-28). Efforts to minimize such compromises can only be undertaken when researchers are embedded enough within the social context of sex-work venues to recognize "slow," or "down," times for sexual commerce in these sites, so that "paying to listen" adds income, rather than presenting an earning conflict for the dancer or sex worker. Compensation in our study—$30 per approximately 30-minute interview—was close to market price for comparable time spent lap-dancing in low-end strip clubs, but did not compensate as would a lap dance in wealthier establishments, and was below market price for more involved sex work. It was for these reasons that we sought to locate times and spaces when "paying to listen" enhanced, and never compromised, earnings.

Managing Team Distress

The research team included several highly experienced researchers, the ethnographic partnership had provided more than a year of preparatory engagement in sex-work settings, and preliminary survey work had been lengthy. Nonetheless, the early weeks of recruitment were characterized by various degrees of anxiety and distress in team members. One team member, very enthusiastic during the planning phase, resigned after his first data collection outing. Even team members with life experiences similar to those of the study participants, and those most accustomed to research with high-risk, marginalized persons, found the extent of violence, hopelessness and despair very high in these interviews. Typically, either little reference is made to the phenomenon of researcher distress in standard research manuals, or it's treated as a simple matter of adequate interviewer training (see Grove et al.). Disciplines outside of public health much more frequently address the "burnout" that comes with working among highly marginalized and distressed populations (for example, see Arrington for coping with stress in social work, and Fearon and Nicol for prevention of burnout among nurses). Despite following the detailed protocols for referring distressed subjects for follow-up support, a team-member pondered the limitations of his role as a researcher:

> July 30th: I surveyed two people. Second scored sky high on all the mental health issues. Said he saw someone get killed, and was clearly very broken up about it...made reportedly a lot of money for his sex work. He was super depressed at his bleak life, not knowing when he was going to die. [...] He was visibly shaken, depressed, and there was this distinct feeling that he was just frustrated and wanted to give up. He was or at least had been suicidal in the past, though now he said he was ok. I went to pay him [his participant fee] and had [the study co-investigator] talk to him, who followed up with him and referred him to [referral] and contacted people at [CSO] about what was going on.... But why do I think that my ability to refer him to someone specific will really do anything useful?

Younger, less experienced team members were paired with senior members, and joked about our check-ins being a little too frequent, perhaps unnecessary. Yet in the course of the ethnographic research during the preceding year, we had learned that distress in junior researchers can build unknowingly; several months into the ethnography, we had recruited a trauma expert from the University Health Services to meet with the team, and the expertise was helpful to all. Despite those lessons, in the course of reviewing our survey process, one young CSO staff team member reflected on moments in which he'd not known how, or whether, he should really interrupt an outing to a venue after gang members had entered the club. This raised for us the recognition that outing leaders needed to routinely review communication strategies for exiting a research venue quickly in the event that any team member recognized signs of potential threat.

Collective Skills, Collective Difficulties

We planned to collect data in groups of two to five team members. Much discussion and reflection (including with the University Ethical Review Board), had gone into a decision to avoid single-person data collection; the University required that no students would undertake research outings alone, but would always work in the company of more experienced researchers. However, there was also an element of "methodological carryover," as we drew upon the positive experience of conducting team ethnography the year before. Bourgois and Schonberg describe the benefits of collaborative ethnography: "[p]articipant-observation is by definition an intensely subjective process ... Collaborators have the advantage of being able to scrutinize one another's contrasting interpretations and insights" (11). We too had begun to understand the value of differing perspectives and differing interpersonal skill sets and demographic categorizations during our year of collaborative ethnography. Given the range of race/ethnicity, sexual orientation, gender presentation, age, Spanish or English fluency, and pre-existing contacts within our team, the heterogeneity of our survey team meant that we were able to access spaces and people that would otherwise have proven difficult.

However, while this diversity proved invaluable, it also provided a unique set of challenges in the field, with researchers occasionally gauging the accessibility of venues differently based on their distinct backgrounds. On a few occasions, such differences made for tense outings. For example, in a venue with known gang affiliation, a team member with experience working with gang members entered only at the behest of another team member. While inside, he proposed a very specific set of behaviors couched in respect for the power dynamic he believed to be at play, and felt that the other team partner was too light-hearted in his approach. Later, both expressed some frustration with the other's chosen style, and the team members were paired off with other members for subsequent outings.

Robins et al. describe such team challenges when bringing together researchers of different epistemological backgrounds, stating "...many difficulties in mixed-methods research are not the result of misunderstandings or points of confusion, but rather emerge from different worldviews that are deeply rooted in the philosophies of knowledge that researchers bring to their work" (728). Many researchers solve such dilemmas by consistently working alone, or in small teams. But heterogeneity within a research team serves an important function in venue-based survey research if those venues differ to the extent that they did in the present project. Our team size, 11 members, worked mostly to our advantage, and was large enough to accommodate many different researcher combinations on different outings. Despite occasional differences (as described above), over the course of the survey, team members learned one another's styles, made some adjustments, and paired off with those with whom they felt most effective.

Potential for Harm

Extensive preparation and team-building reduces the risks of human error and harm, but the process is not foolproof. Soliciting information from participants whose behaviors put them at legal risk, or at risk for public disapproval and stigma, raises multiple opportunities for researchers to cause harm to participants and to themselves. Moral challenges abound in the nature of questions asked, and whether or not such questions contribute to what Goffman describes as the "spoiled identity" or the "mortification of self." As mentioned earlier, young people occasionally displayed signs of distress during an interview, particularly in response to questions regarding childhood, for which there was much evidence of fragile families and personal loss. While the survey team had clear lines of procedure and protocols for referral in such cases, the extent and effectiveness of follow-up was usually not known to the researchers.

There was also a possible risk of association for a participant—in other words, potential risk for simply talking to a research team member and/or completing the survey. These risks might include interrogation or exploitation by club managers or hostility from fellow dancers. For instance, while in most clubs we worked *through* owners and managers to gain entry, on several occasions we had prior alliances with women working a club, and planned *with them* how to recruit others. This was possible because club managers don't typically employ dancers (dancers have permission to dance in a given club, and provide the owner some portion of their tips), meaning the dancers are freelance workers. The risk this latter method of sampling incurred, however, was that the manager may have questioned the dancers about the interviews after we left the venue, or may have required each dancer to hand over some fraction of the extra $30 they knew she had earned for participating in the survey. Hostility between dancers could also have been heightened due to variations in eligibility for the survey, especially given that many of the women reported existing tensions between themselves and other dancers during the interview. Other sources of stress or hostility might include bouncers and others. Yet, our gauge was always the participants themselves—if they wanted to take part in the study, and could make it work for them, we assumed they knew it could work to their advantage.

Relying on that gauge, however, may be problematic when dealing with drug-addicted participants. Crack- or heroin-addicted sex workers have a different threshold of risk brought on by their addiction, raising unique ethical questions. In the course of interviewing a group of 15-20 women selling sex on the street over a few days near a fast-food restaurant, we gradually realized that most of them were daily users of heroin and/or cocaine. We also gradually learned, in the course of our interviews, that they were shunned not only by the restaurant where we were parked, but by most of the merchants on that stretch of road. Yet this was their beat, and without transport or the means to ride buses, this was the extent of their geographic reach. This research site raised the delicate question of where street venues start and end (at the edge of parking lots? adjacent public parks?), and whether sex workers working the street are the "community" to approve recruitment in public spaces, or whether the geographic scope of permissions sought should extend more widely into neighboring businesses.

Potential harm to team members also includes "courtesy stigma," or the stigma by association (Phillips et al.) of being seen in select clubs, or with sex workers or known addicts. Goffman suggests that stigmas of the "spoiled self" affect those working closely with stigmatized individuals or groups. In the latter cases, these associations can be so automatic that they are not moderated by one's attitude about the stigma (Pryor, Reeder and Monroe). That is, no matter one's specific attitude about sex workers and drug users, the stigma applied to those seen associating with them may be automatic. In the narrative below, three women passed by as we chatted with a sex worker who had just completed a transaction in a parked truck across the block. In sidelong glances and glares of disapproval, they communicated to us the courtesy stigma of being seen alongside a woman whose presentation spoke of drug use and sex work:

> August 15, 2012: While we sat on the curb with [her], a group of about three women came out of a car from the parking lot behind us and looked at [the other team-member] and me. They said, "you know she is a girl right?". Clear as day, they were trying to tell us […] that we were talking with someone that sells sex.

Indeed, in the course of reviewing our process for this paper, one of our team members who lives in Detroit discussed his concerns over courtesy stigma from anyone who may have seen him conducting interviews:

> People who you may know from other settings may not be able to appreciate or understand the reason you are there... with a person who is obviously identifiable in the community as a sex worker, and in a context where explaining one's reasoning for sitting with such a person is unallowable.

This reaction underscores the challenge of courtesy stigma in research that reaches across multiple social and geographic locations and responds, in real time, to new opportunities on the street: such approaches heighten the chance that boundaries may overlap.

We likewise had to navigate outright prejudice directed towards participants, often while simultaneously needing the assistance of those perpetrating the discrimination. We frequently made small talk with employees in venues in which we interviewed. In one instance, two team members were having a discussion with the parking lot attendant outside a local bar:

> August 15th: [Name], the guy watching the parking lot, kept referring to [the women selling outside of the bar] as drug users, his exact words escape me, but I think it was "crack whores," and he...doesn't give them a light. It is odd to pay him more [money] than I would otherwise pay a parking lot guy because I need him to watch my car, when he so clearly discriminates with vitriol against the very group we are trying to empower.

Sustaining Relationships

While the DYP research project is designed to improve services in Detroit and elsewhere, and new spin-off projects may indeed serve the populations that were represented by the participants in this research, the friendships with participants cannot be easily sustained, given that we operate in a research culture of protected identities and confidentiality. Protecting participant identity is an essential element of behavioral research ethics, yet such requirements foster relationships that can seem inhumanely aborted at the end of an interview. Our shared team-briefings have highlighted the distress among team members over having no approved means to re-connect, or sustain the relationships, with specific participants who shared so much. This has heightened motivations for spin-off projects that have potential good, but it also places in stark relief the distinct goals of the community partner agencies (CBOs), and the research university. While partner agencies are building rapport and looking for sustained *personal* relationships of service, the researchers—having agreed to protocols of non-contact—are left wondering about participants they cannot re-locate, or with whom they cannot check in.

Potential for Good

Possibly the most significant, overarching challenge is what good the research can offer to participants, and to community partners actively engaged in direct services to communities of young people. Titling this article "Paying to Listen" marks our explicit effort to centralize ethical listening as a bridge across degrees of social separation between not only young participants and researchers, but also between the members of a heterogeneous survey team that represent academia, community outreach, and activism. Ethical listening (Beard) is a prerequisite for progressive learning, and is an essential dimension of critical race and ethnic studies, feminist research, queer studies, and cultural or public health research that pursues scholarship as a vehicle for social justice. As Dewey wrote in his early arguments for progressive education, "…communication is educative. One shares in what another has thought and felt, and in so doing … has his own attitude modified" (10).

"Paying to listen" appeared to offer social value to participants. The value of simply having someone "hear my story" was a theme that emerged repeatedly from participants in the course of our interviews, and the more stigmatized a particular participant's circumstance, the more s/he valued the conversation. Often, being paid $30 to talk rather than perform sexual services was a welcome change for participants, and many relaxed into the exchange, sharing more of their personal narrative than the survey questions required. The following field notes capture this kind of exchange:

> August 13th: Each of the first three subjects fall asleep during the interview—at first I think it's a manifestation of drug use, but I think it's that plus something else—they're letting down for the first time in a while… a message on the stress in their lives… to sit here, in a safe space with a kindly middle-age woman who wants to hear their story… they begin to unwind, they laugh a bit, but each of them cry at times and I cry with them, they breathe deeper, drift off. I give them a few minutes and then

gently ask another question… we go on. They seem so grateful for the interview—not the money, but yes that too—but the talk, the chance to be with anyone who's safe; they don't want to get out of the car when [the interview] is over.

Despite the potential immediate benefits of "safe" conversation, however, many of the team members who were accustomed to participating in direct community outreach for clinical care felt that the long-term benefits to participants seemed remote. There is certainly the potential for programs and services to be developed from information gained in the survey, but there is no way to ensure that the individuals interviewed will receive these services, or even know that they exist, once developed.

True to the intention of our community collaboration, however, all research lessons learned feed back directly into the work of the three community partner agencies, and are designed to enrich their activities. Thanks to the project's sponsor, the Ford Foundation, Detroit Youth Passages also has an explicit emphasis on follow-up and communication, and several new partnerships have allowed us to concretize ways that the team can "give back" to the communities we've been researching. Foremost among these is a new spin-off project on social enterprise—reviewing successful social and micro-enterprise projects in the city and in the US broadly, to design a project of this type to serve residentially unstable youth, especially those engaged in sexual commerce. A national conference is planned in Detroit in 2013, during which keynote speakers from US projects will share their successes, DYP survey data on needs and potential skills will be featured, and youth will participate. The goal of the conference is to design a model for job creation among those served by our respective partner organizations. Donor responses to the proposed project have been encouraging to date, and we are additionally proposing to a local philanthropist the creation of housing for drug-addicted youth.

The research itself contains potential for both direct and indirect good both for participant populations and team members. Data generated on the social vulnerabilities, employment circumstances, and aspirations of Detroit youth provide publishable, empirical evidence of circumstances long-understood by our partner organizations, generating data that can strengthen advocacy among public and private sector opinion-leaders, policy-makers and donors. As a venue-based survey that reached across numerous diverse neighborhoods, the survey highlights geographic patterns of heightened self-reported stress, violence and drug use, affirming areas of greater vulnerability for youth within the sexual commerce and entertainment industry.

While we were troubled by our inability to sustain contact with individual participants, we were encouraged by the opportunity provided by the survey to promote linkages between participants and the community organizations, tailored to needs reported within the survey itself; e.g. needs for services addressing mental health, housing, or drug use. At the close of each interview, we shared a referral sheet with the contact information of our three partner organizations, and could speak to the specific needs identified in the survey. One team member reflected that he saw many participants pursue HIV testing and health services as a result of participating in the interview. He also noted that the interviews and the listening exchange provided him with "educational opportunities" in which he was able to discuss how to transition from exchanging sex on the street to safer work. That this came from a young man who had himself transitioned from exchanging sex to a student employed as a public health researcher serves as a powerful example of the potentially transformative power of ethical listening and shared progressive learning in academic and community-based collaborations.

Endnotes

1. "Progressive Learning" references the values inherent in the Progressive Education movement, i.e. the promotion of learning that emphasizes the development of critical thinking, respect for diversity, and the democratic ideals of social and political inclusiveness. See Westbrook, R.B. (1991) for a discussion of John Dewey's (1916) philosophy of progressive education for engaged citizenship and social justice.

2. See Bolton: "Because of the restrictions surrounding sex, [a] 'feel' for the phenomenon may be of exceptional importance when studying sexual behavior" (148).

Works Cited

Arrington, Perétte. *Stress at work: How do social workers cope?* NASW Membership Workforce Study. Washington, DC: National Association of Social Workers, 2008. PDF file.

Beard, David. "A Broader Understanding of the Ethics of Listening: Philosophy, Cultural Studies, Media Studies and the Ethical Listening Subject." *International Journal of Listening*, 23.1 (2009): 7-20. Print.

Berardi, Gigi. "Application of Participatory Rural Appraisal in Alaska." *Human Organization*. 57.4 (1998): 438-46. Print.

Bolton, Ralph. "Mapping Terra Incognita: Sex Research for AIDS Prevention – An Urgent Agenda for the 1990s." 1992. *Sexualities: Critical Concepts in Sociology*. Ed. Kenneth Plummer. London, New York: Routledge. Print.

Bourgois, Philippe I. and Jeff Schonberg. *Righteous Dopefiend*. Berkeley, California: University of California Press, 2009. Print.

Couch, Jen, Ben Durant and Jennifer Hill. "Young People, Old Issues: Methodological Concerns in Research with Highly Marginalised Young People." *Youth Studies Australia*, 31.4 (2012): 46-54. Print.

Dalla, Rochelle L. "Et tu Brute? A Qualitative Analysis of Streetwalking Prostitutes' Interpersonal Support Networks." *Journal of Family Issues* 22 (2001): 1066-85. Print.

Dalla Rochelle L., Yan Xia and Heather Kennedy. "'You Just Give Them What They Want and Pray They Don't Kill You': Street-level Sex Workers Reports of Victimization, Personal Resources, and Coping Strategies." *Violence against Women* 9.11 (2003): 1367-94.

Dewey John. *Democracy and Education: An Introduction to a Philosophy of Education*. 1916. New York: The Free Press, 1966. Print.

Earls, Christopher M. and Hélène David. "Male and Female Prostitution: A Review." *Annals of Sex Abuse* 2.1 (1989): 5-28. Print.

Elias, James E., Vera L. Bullough, Veronica Elias and Gwen Brewer. "Doing Research with Sex Workers." *Prostitution: On Whores, Hustlers and Johns*. Ed. James E. Elias, Vera L. Bullough, Veronica Elias and Gwen Brewer. Amherst, New York: Prometheus Books, 1998. Print.

Fearon, C. and M. Nicol. "Strategies to Assist Prevention of Burnout in Nursing Staff." *Nursing Standard* 26.14 (2011): 35-39. Print.

Flowers, Amy. "Research from Within: Participant Observation in the Phone-sex Workplace." *Prostitution: On Whores, Hustlers and Johns*. Ed. James E. Elias, Vera L. Bullough, Veronica Elias and Gwen Brewer. Amherst, New York: Prometheus Books, 1998. Print.

Goffman, Erving. *Stigma: Notes on the Management of Spoiled Identity*. Englewood Cliffs, New Jersey: Prentice Hall, 1963. Print.

Gorry, Jo, Katrina Roen and James Reilly. "Selling Your Self? The Psychological Impact of Street Sex Work and Factors Affecting Support Seeking." *Health and Social Care in the Community* 18.5 (2010): 492-499. Print.

Groves, Robert M., Floyd J. Fowler, Mick Couper, James M. Lepkowski, Eleanor Singer and Roger Tourangeau. *Survey Methodology*. 2nd ed. Hoboken, New Jersey: Wiley, 2009. Print.

Grudzen, Corita R., Daniella Meeker, Jacqueline M. Torres, Qingling Du, R. Sean Morrison, Ronald M. Andersen and Lillian Gelberg. "Comparison of Mental Health of Female Adult Film Performers and Other Young Women in California." *Psychiatric Services* 62.6 (2011): 639-645. Print.

Harding, Sandra. "Is There a Feminist Method?" *Feminisms*. Ed. Sandra Kemp and Judith Squires. Oxford: Oxford University Press, 1986.

Holloway, Wendy and Tony Jefferson. *Doing Qualitative Research Differently: Free Association, Narrative and the Interview Method*. London & Thousand Oaks, CA: Sage Publications, 2000. Print.

Hubbard, Phil. "Researching Female Sex Work: Reflections on Geographical Exclusion, Critical Methodologies and 'Useful' Knowledge." *Area* 31.3 (1999): 229-37. Print.

Israel, Barbara, Amy J. Schultz, Edith A. Parker and Adam B. Becker. "Review of Community-based Research: Assessing Partnership Approaches to Improve Public Health." *Annual Rev Public Health*, 19.1 (1998): 173-202. Print.

Jeal, N., and C. Salisbury. "Health Needs and Service Use of Parlour-based Prostitutes Compared with Street-based Prostitutes: A Cross-sectional Study." *British Journal of Obstetrics and Gynecology* 114.7 (2007): 875-81. Print.

Keeling, Kara and Josh Kun. "Introduction: Listening to American Studies." *American Quarterly* 63.3 (2011): 445-459. Print.

Kinsey, Alfred C., Wardell B. Pomeroy and Clyde E. Martin. *Sexual Behavior in the Human Male*. Philadelphia: W.B. Saunders, 1948. Print.

Kinsey, Alfred C., Wardell B. Pomeroy, Clyde E. Martin and Paul H. Gebhard. *Sexual Behavior in the Human Female*. Indianapolis, IN: Indiana University Press, 1953. Print.

Lantz, P.M., E. Viruell-Fuentes, B.A. Israel, D. Softley and R. Guzman. "Can Communities and Academia Work Together on Public Health Research? Evaluation Results from a Community-Based Participatory Research Partnership in Detroit." *Journal of Urban Health: Bulletin of the New York Academy of Medicine* 78.3 (2001): 495-507. Print.

Liamputtong, Pranee. *Researching the Vulnerable: A Guide to Sensitive Research Methods*. London: Sage Publications, 2007. Print.

Link, Bruce G. and Jo C. Phelan. "Conceptualizing Stigma." *Annual Review of Sociology* 27 (2001): 363-85. Print.

Martinez-Ebers, Valerie. "Using Monetary Incentives with Hard-to-reach Populations in Panel Surveys." *International Journal of Public Opinion Research* 9.1 (1997): 77-86. Print.

Phillips Rachel, Cecilia Benoit, Helga Hallgrimsdottir and Kate Vallance. "Courtesy Stigma: A Hidden Health Concern among Front-line Service Providers to Sex Workers." *Sociology of Health and Illness* 34.5 (2012): 681-96. Print.

Pryor, John B., Glenn D. Reeder and Andrew E. Monroe. "The Infection of Bad Company: Stigma by Association." *Journal of Personality and Social Psychology* 102.2 (2012): 224–41. Print.

Remple Valencia P., Caitlin Johnston, David M. Patrick, Mark W. Tyndall and Ann M. Jolly. "Conducting HIV/AIDS research with indoor commercial sex workers: Researching a hidden population." *Progress in Community Health Partnerships: Research, Education, and Action* 1.2 (2007): 161-8. Print.

Rickard, Wendy. "Talking Lived Reality: Using Oral History to Record a More Balanced History of Sex Work." *Prostitution: On Whores, Hustlers and Johns*. Ed. James E. Elias, Vera L. Bullough, Veronica Elias and Gwen Brewer. Amherst, New York: Prometheus Books, 1998. Print.

Robins, Cynthia S., Norma C. Ware, Susan dos Reis, Cathleen E. Willging, Joyce Y. Chung and Roberto Lewis-Fernández. "Dialogues on Mixed-Methods and Mental Health Services Research: Anticipating Challenges, Building Solutions." *Psychiatr Serv.* 59.7 (2008): 727–31. Print.

Rossler, W., U. Koch, C. Lauber, A.K. Hass, M. Altwegg, V. Ajdacic-Gross and K. Landolt. "The Mental Health of Female Sex Workers." *Acta Psychiactra Scandinavica* 122 (2010): 143-152. Print.

Seymour, Craig. "Studying Myself/ Studying Others: One (Professional) Boy's Adventures Studying Sex Work." *Prostitution: On Whores, Hustlers and Johns*. Ed. James E. Elias, Vera L. Bullough, Veronica Elias and Gwen Brewer. Amherst, New York: Prometheus Books, 1998. Print.

Shaver, Frances M. "Sex Work Research: Methodological and Ethical Challenges." *Journal of Interpersonal Violence* 20.3 (2005): 296-319. Print.

Wahab, Stéphanie. "Creating Knowledge Collaboratively with Female Sex Workers: Insights from a Qualitative, Feminist, and Participatory Study." *Qualitative Inquiry* 9.4 (2003): 625-42. Print.

Weitzer, Ronald. "Flawed Theory and Method in Studies of Prostitution". *Violence against Women* 11.7 (2005): 934. Print.

———. "New Directions in Research on Prostitution." *Crime, Law & Social Change* 43 (2005): 211-235. Print.

Westbrook, Robert B. *John Dewey and American Democracy.* Ithaca and London: Cornell University Press, 1991. Print.

Rachel Snow, Ph.D., Associate Professor of Health Behavior and Health Education, University of Michigan (at time of writing) (rsnow@unfpa.org); Angela M. Williams, MPH., University of Michigan (at time of writing) (williamsangm@gmail.com); Curtis Collins (curtiscollins17@gmail.com); Jessica Moorman, MHS, Department of Communication Studies, University of Michigan (moorman@umich.edu); Tomas Rangel (trangel174@yahoo.com); Audrey Barick, MPH, University of Michigan (abarick@umich.edu); Crystal Clay (crystal_clay629@yahoo.com); Armando Matiz Reyes, DDS, University of Michigan (armandom@umich.edu).

Moving Past Assumptions: Recognizing Parents as Allies in Promoting the Sexual Literacies of Adolescents through a University-Community Collaboration

Stacey S. Horn, Christina R. Peter, Timothy B. Tasker, and Shannon Sullivan

This article recounts how a university-community collaborative challenged prevailing assumptions about parents as barriers to the provision of gender and sexuality information to their children, allowing for the recognition of parents as critical stakeholders and partners in sexual literacy work with youth. We provide evidence that parents' support for inclusive sexuality education uniquely situates them to educate and advocate for young people around these issues, and in so doing we hope to disrupt the rhetoric that casts parents in the United States as solely gatekeepers when it comes to young people's access to information about the broad spectrum of human sexuality.

In 2010, our ongoing university-community collaboration initiated a new research project to explore the ways that young people make sense of gender and sexuality, and the role that schools play in channeling, supporting, and challenging young peoples' emerging understandings of these issues. The collaborative project, called Project Safe SPACES (Social Pressures, Attitudes, Culture and Experiences related to Sexuality), grew out of a long-time research and practice partnership between a university researcher and the Executive Director of a community-based organization (CBO). This partnership helped to further the CBO's mission to "promote the safety, support, and healthy development for lesbian, gay, bisexual, transgender, and questioning (LGBTQ) youth in Illinois schools and communities, through advocacy, education, youth organizing, and research." Project Safe SPACES is the most recent instantiation of our ongoing collaboration. This particular project was made possible through a grant program funded by the Ford Foundation that was focused on using research, graduate training, and strategic communications to advance the public conversation on adolescent sexual health and sexual rights within the United States.

The funding and support provided by that grant allowed us to both deepen and expand on the existing collaboration in two important ways. First, our collaboration was able to incorporate graduate students and graduate training more fully into the work that we were doing, offering invaluable experience to the next generation of sexuality and community-based researchers. Second, this project led to the establishment of a community advisory board (CAB), which has partnered with us on every aspect of the project, from the design of surveys and interview protocols, through the development of communication strategies, to the dissemination of findings to key stakeholders. Currently, the Project Safe SPACES collaborative consists of: a university-based research team (comprising faculty and graduate students in educational psychology, human development, community psychology, elementary education, and youth development); a statewide community-based safe schools organization; and, importantly, a CAB consisting of parents, teachers, young people, youth advocates, sexuality educators, public health experts, and other researchers.

Similarly, the grant program required us to embed strategic communication practices into all of the aforementioned stages of the project. A key aspect of our strategic communication work involved attending to the variety of audiences that have a stake in decision-making processes regarding issues of young peoples' sexuality, sexual health, and sexual literacies, both within and outside of school. In addition, our strategic communication approach includes an ongoing focus on "messaging" the research results in ways that are accessible to persons within the broader community, in the hopes of effecting positive change for young people throughout the state of Illinois. These aspects of our strategic communication plan are apparent in our collaborative, long-term vision statement:

> The vision of Project Safe SPACES is that school communities in Illinois will be safe, supportive, and transformative places for all young people regardless of gender, gender identity/expression, and/or sexuality. In order to do this we need to decrease the prevalence of peer harassment that is related to gender, sex, and sexuality. This project aims to do this by investigating the individual, developmental, and contextual factors related to gender- and sexuality-based harassment and to use the results of this research to create contexts and school cultures in which people talk about gender, sex, and sexuality and grapple with the complexity of these issues in structured (traditional), non-structured, supported, developmentally appropriate, and safe ways.

Our collaboration recognized early on that, although we had focused much attention on reducing peer-to-peer sexuality- and gender-based harassment, we had yet to consider the kinds of spaces we wanted schools to be. Retaining this type of deficit framework would, in turn, have limited the kinds of questions we might ask, the information our work might generate, and how that information could inform advocacy and policy. These realizations led us to incorporate more of an asset-based framing into our vision. As a result, we reconceptualized gender- and sexuality-based harassment as it is situated within a school culture that tends to constrain young peoples' conversations about gender, sex, and sexuality to particular spaces (e.g., health class) and concepts (e.g., abstinence until marriage) and within particular frames (e.g., compulsory heterosexuality, sexuality education as disease and/or pregnancy prevention). This containment, in turn, serves to narrow young peoples' meaning-making around their developing gendered and sexual selves, and limits the legibility of an array of sexual literacies. We therefore came to view as essential to our work the transformation of schools into places that both allowed young people to grapple with and develop their sexual literacies, and also supported these processes through the school's own policies, programs, practices, and community collaborations.

Also as part of the early strategic communications work, we developed an audience matrix to identify key stakeholder groups that we thought would help us to achieve our vision, as well as those that could create barriers for creating safe spaces for sexual literacy education. One of the first stakeholder groups that we identified was parents, and we identified them as barriers. When developing the matrix, however, we realized that we had based our assumption that parents were barriers on the perceptions and experiences of a small subset of our group, but not on the actual beliefs of parents themselves. We came to acknowledge that we knew very little about what parents thought about schools being places "in which people talk about gender, sex, and sexuality and grapple with the complexity of these issues in structured (traditional), non-structured, supported, developmentally appropriate, and safe ways" in three specific ways. First, we knew very little about parents' views regarding young peoples' understanding of their sexuality and sexual health. Second, we realized that we did not understand parents' views of young peoples' access to sexual literacy knowledge, particularly around knowledges that may be viewed as more controversial. Our collaborative simply did not know what parents' attitudes were regarding the appropriateness of several domains of sexual literacies such as sexual orientation, gender identity, and issues related to sexual desire and pleasure.

Finally, we realized that educators in schools represent only one of several key sexual literacy facilitators young people encounter, yet we did not know whether parents viewed those other community members as appropriate facilitators of sexual literacy. Importantly, we also realized that we barely acknowledged, let alone understood, the role that parents do and should play as facilitators of and partners in the developing sexual literacies of their children. The realization that we knew so little about these issues prompted us to add a component to Project Safe SPACES that involved systematically investigating parental attitudes about the roles that they themselves, schools, and various other community members should play in educating young people about sexual health, sexual desire and pleasure, sexual identity, and gender identity and expression.

Accordingly, the purpose of this article is to tell the story of the journey through which we transformed our assumptions about parents being simply obstacles to progressive approaches to inclusive sexuality education. The perspective that has emerged is one in which we view parents as critical stakeholders and partners in the work of facilitating young people's sexual literacy development. Through telling our very local story, we also hope to disrupt the predominant national rhetoric that casts parents in the U.S. as conservative gatekeepers when it comes to young people's access to the knowledges that reflect the broad spectrum of human sexuality. In addition, we provide evidence that parents are uniquely situated to make inclusive sexuality education accessible to young people, both in terms of being young peoples' first and primary sexuality educators, but also in terms of advocating for practices and policies regarding the types of sexual knowledges and sexual literacies included within schools. In the pages that follow, we further detail the process by which we came to reframe parents as allies in promoting sexual literacies for adolescents. Through recounting our own progression on these issues, we also hope to encourage other researchers to challenge their own assumptions.

What We Did

Because of the diverse partners involved in our collaborative, this systematic investigation played out in unique and important ways that drew upon the expertise, resources, and knowledges of all participants within the Safe SPACES partnership. Through an iterative and collaborative process, we designed a project that would not only generate systematic, empirical knowledge regarding parents' attitudes, but would also build upon the knowledge of those more directly engaged in the work of educating and advocating for young people. Through our collective conversations regarding the project, we recognized the need for evidence regarding parental attitudes and beliefs about inclusive sexuality education that was more than simply anecdotal. Further, the community advocates on the CAB emphasized the importance of having access to proximal and local data, rather than national data, or data from other states, in working with decision-makers in schools and communities.

From this starting point, the university-based research team then employed the resources of the academy to identify what the empirical knowledge base could offer about parental attitudes regarding education around a variety of domains of sexuality knowledge. It was apparent in the research literature that access to broad information and open communication about sexuality and sexual health was associated with healthier sexuality outcomes among adolescents, and therefore constituted best practices (Institute of Medicine; Jaccard, Dittus, and Gordon). These evidence-based strategies are most aligned with a comprehensive sexuality education curriculum in formal educational contexts. Though comprehensiveness is used to refer to the inclusion of a variety of domains of sexual health topics (such as sexual risks and protections), there have been calls to include topics relevant to relationships, pleasure, and sexual and gender identity to further support healthy sexuality for a diversity of young people (Allen; Society for Adolescent Medicine). Despite these calls for more inclusive and comprehensive sexuality education for young people, students rarely receive a comprehensive curriculum in schools (Landry, Kaeser, and Richards; National Guidelines Task Force).

In order to understand this disconnect between best and prevailing practices, the research team again consulted the literature to identify key barriers to implementing comprehensive sexuality education. In U.S. schools broadly, a significant barrier has been government proscriptions through federal funding guidelines. Federal funds have been provided only to schools and community programs that deliver exclusively abstinence-only sexuality curricula (Solomon-Fears 13). These funding limitations started with The Adolescent Family Life Program (Title XX of the Public Health Services Act, *Public Law No. 97-35, 1981*) and are evident in other programs such as the Personal Responsibility and Work Opportunity Reconciliation Act of 1996 (welfare reform law, P.L 104-193) and the Community-Based Abstinence Education Grant Program, under title XI, Section 1110 of the Social Security Act.

The Department of Health and Human Services, for instance, offered grants under Title XI, Section 1110 of the Social Security Act to programs that adhered to strict abstinence-only messaging and taught abstinence before marriage as "the expected standard of human sexual activity" (Catalog of Federal Domestic Assistance). Furthermore, these funds were restricted to abstinence-only education that explicitly stated that sexual activity outside of marriage is likely to be psychologically and physically harmful to the individual, his or her parents, and his or her society, in keeping with the language of Section 510(b)(2) of Title V of the Social Security Act. Accordingly, programs that "promote the use of contraceptives" were not eligible for this type of funding, further silencing a critical component of the comprehensive sexuality conversation. Though the Community-Based Abstinence Education Grant Program was discontinued in fiscal year 2010, no monies have been earmarked for programs that use truly inclusive and comprehensive sexuality curricula, despite extant research findings reflecting healthier outcomes for youth who receive such programming (Kirby). Further, federal grants for abstinence-only programs, through the aforementioned welfare reform law (P.L 104-193), have been renewed through the year 2014 under P.L. 111-148.

These types of funding regulations and restrictions, in essence, shape the sexuality narratives that schools and communities are allowed to provide students, and serve to censor or limit the sexual literacies to which young people are exposed in schools. As a consequence, young people bear greater responsibility for identifying and accessing more complete sexual literacies. Traditionally, young people then turn to parents, peers, and media to fully develop these literacies (Allen). In summary, abstinence-only policies have constrained the range of the conversation around sexuality and sexual health for young people. These types of messages not only frame sexuality and sexual activity in very limited ways (e.g., partnered sexual intercourse), they also serve to silence the experiences of a large percentage of young people (e.g., those who identify as lesbian or gay, for whom marriage is not always an option; those who do not wish to marry; those who are already sexually active; those who are pregnant or parenting) and thus render as unimportant sexual knowledges and literacies that fall outside of these heteronormative, traditional, and limited scripts.

Despite the long-standing federal support for abstinence-only education, since 2010 a shift has begun to occur. The U.S. government has begun supporting evidence-based programming through federal funding that aims to reduce teen and "out-of-wedlock" pregnancy for youth without adhering strictly to abstinence messaging. Specifically, recent federal funding provides monetary support exclusively for programs that offer comprehensive sexuality education (Solomon-Fears 9). Further, programming aimed at reducing teen pregnancy through providing "medically accurate and age appropriate" information became eligible for funding under the Teen Pregnancy Prevention Program (P.L. 111-117), starting in 2010. More recently, the Patient Protection and Affordable Care Act of 2010 (P.L. 111-148), while restoring funding for abstinence programming, also provides $375 million in funding over five years to allow states to take a comprehensive approach to pregnancy and STD prevention by providing information about topics such as contraception and healthy relationships, in addition to abstinence. While this shift in government funding allows for further implementation of effective comprehensive sexuality education programs, and facilitates the promotion of an expanded sexuality narrative in schools, its focus is still limited primarily to the prevention of disease and pregnancy. Unfortunately, comprehensive sexuality education has yet to be realized in all schools and communities. The continued offerings of abstinence education in many schools, in light of these shifting governmental supports, caused us to reflect on the roles that both schools and parents play in shaping sexual literacies. Many educators and advocates fear that comprehensive and progressive approaches will be met with resistance, particularly from parents (Eisenberg, et al.). The current existence of funding for two distinct forms of sexuality education in schools makes understanding parents' attitudes toward various forms of sexuality education curricula and sexual literacy topics an imperative.

Such work could shed light on discrepancies that exist in the research literature. For instance, some research suggests that school educators and administrators view parents as potential barriers to providing this more inclusive form of sexuality and health information (Eisenberg, et al.). In contrast, other research demonstrates that parents often serve as providers of comprehensive sexuality information for their children and that parents endorse the involvement of schools and community members as partners in this work (Alexander and Jorgenson; Byers, Sears, and Weaver; Constantine, Jerman, and Huang). Research in this vein concludes that opposition seems to come from only a vocal minority of parents (Jorgensen and Alexander). These parental voices are diminished, however, when we rely solely on the assumptions of school administrators and policy-makers regarding parental involvement, instead of gathering empirical evidence about such attitudes from parents themselves. As a consequence, youth continue to receive limited information about sexuality and sexual health in schools.

Developing sexuality literacy need not be limited to formal educational contexts. In fact, while research suggests that young people think their parents should be a primary source of knowledge about sexuality, both parents and young people believe that peers and the media are often the sources from which young people are developing their sexual literacies (Lagus et al.; Secor-Turner, Sieving, Eisenberg, and Skay; Somers and Surmann). This suggests that both parents and young people recognize that youth actively seek more knowledge than is currently offered in formal sexuality education contexts.

The literature summarized here suggests that parents support some components of sexuality education for their children, likely viewing themselves as primary participants in this process, but still recognize and rely on other community members to support young peoples' development of sexual literacy. What remains yet unknown is whether parents also endorse the inclusion of information about particular domains of sexual knowledge – such as relationships, pleasure, and sexual and gender identity – within a comprehensive framework. Moreover, we do not know whether the findings of earlier research hold true for Illinois parents broadly, as well as for parents from diverse ethnic, cultural, and religious groups. Finally, because these topics have been largely neglected in past research, the ages at which parents believe young people are ready to start these conversations, and the role of other community members in these conversations, also remain unknown.

In view of the aforementioned research, and the significant gaps that remain in the literature, the research team subsequently developed the first draft of a survey directed at uncovering parental attitudes about a wide array of sexuality education topics reflecting the broad spectrum of human sexuality. Importantly, a primary focus of grant funding from the Ford Foundation that supported our work was the sexual health and sexual rights of young people. In keeping with this framework, our work was further informed by the World Health Organization's definition of these constructs.[1] Notably, we were interested in framing sexuality as a positive aspect of one's individual identity, as well as of the broader human experience. Further, we wanted to ensure that we operated from definitions of sexual health and sexual rights that situated sexuality, and sexual identity, as critical to the development of the self – the psychological and physical integrity of the person – and over which young people should not only have agency, but also primary control. Together, these definitions and the existing research literature guided the initial questions and focal topics for our survey: we became interested in the inclusion of topics such as sexual pleasure, sexual agency, masturbation, romantic relationships, sexual orientation, and gender identity, which move the conversation of sexual literacies beyond disease and pregnancy prevention.

The research team also recognized the benefits of diverse perspectives represented on the CAB when developing and refining the measures that were used in the study. Accordingly, the research team presented an initial draft of the survey to the other members of the CAB at a meeting and sought their feedback. Starting with the first draft, various members of the CAB challenged everything from the phrasing of questions to the specific words chosen to represent various sexual literacy topics. In addition, CAB members raised concerns about whether or not specific survey items and topics would be understood, or convey the same meaning, to parents in varying communities across Illinois. Based on these conversations, the research team then refined the survey and brought it back to the entire CAB two additional times for further collaborative review.

The extent to which specific items and topics were refined differed greatly. Though some revisions simply called for changing technical, research language to wording that was more familiar to parents, others required the CAB to explicitly identify which specific sexual literacy concepts were most central to the goals of the research project. As an example of changes that involved revising technical language, earlier drafts of the survey had included the topics of "sexual decision-making" and "sexual agency." During collaborative reviews, CAB members commented that both of these topics were abstract and ambiguous, particularly "sexual agency." Through further deliberation, the collaborative decided that "sexual decision-making" could encompass both ideas, and would be more readily familiar to parents; "sexual agency" was removed. In addition, the collaborative advocated for adding further clarification to "sexual decision-making" by expanding the wording of that topic to include "such as when to become sexually active" (see Table 1).

In contrast, the initial inclusion of topics such as abortion engendered detailed and prolonged discussions regarding the controversial nature of some sexual literacy topics, as well as the set of values that might be implied by their wording. In our initial version, for instance, we included "abortion" as a topic, but did not include pregnancy or parenting. Members of the CAB worried that including only abortion constituted a limited and negative understanding of pregnancy for young people. The CAB recognized early on that the phrasing of concepts around pregnancy implicitly communicated assumptions about the normative timing of these experiences, as well as about young peoples' reproductive agency and decision-making power. Many of the alternative phrases that were considered reflected this tension between normative timing and youth agency: "options for unplanned pregnancy," "pregnancy and choice," "family planning," "what to do if you get pregnant," "options for teen pregnancy," "options for pregnancy," and "unplanned pregnancy/family planning." In the end, the CAB felt that words like "family planning" and "choice" were perhaps too euphemistic and ambiguous. Moreover, inclusion of adjectives like "teen" and "unplanned" appeared to reflect a set of cultural values and assumptions that might not be widely shared, as they cast young people's pregnancies as both different and negative. As a result of these conversations, the collaborative refined the survey to include not only the topic of abortion, but also "pregnancy" and "parenting," capturing concepts related to pregnancy more completely, and in a less biased manner (see Table 1).

Table 1: Revisions to sexual literacy topics based on Community Advisory Board feedback

Initial draft reviewed by CAB	1st revision based on CAB feedback	2nd revision based on CAB feedback	Final items and order
Their bodies	Their bodies	Their bodies (puberty and pubertal changes)	Their bodies (puberty and pubertal changes)
Love	Love	Romantic love	Romantic love
Dating	Dating	Dating	Dating
Dating violence	Dating violence	Dating violence	Dating violence
(absent)	Marriage	Marriage	Marriage
Heterosexuality	Heterosexuality	Heterosexuality	Heterosexuality
Same-sex sexuality	Same-sex sexuality	Same-sex sexuality and bisexuality	Same-sex sexuality and bisexuality
(absent)	(absent)	Gender roles (masculine and feminine)	Gender roles (masculine and feminine)
(absent)	Gender identity	Transgender identity	Transgender identity
Sexual abstinence	Sexual abstinence	Sexual abstinence	Abstaining from sexual activity
Sexual decision-making	Sexual decision-making	Sexual decision-making such as when to become sexually active	Sexual decision-making such as when to become sexually active
Sexual pleasure	Sexual pleasure	Sexual pleasure	Sexual pleasure
Masturbation	Masturbation	Masturbation	Masturbation
Sexually transmitted diseases and infections	Sexually transmitted diseases and infections	Sexual health (sexually transmitted diseases and infections)	Sexually transmitted diseases and infections

Contraception and birth control	Contraception and birth control	Contraception and birth control	Sexual protection (contraception and birth control)
(absent)	Options for teen pregnancy	Options for teen pregnancy	Pregnancy
(absent)	(absent)	(absent)	Parenting
Abortion	Abortion	Abortion	Abortion
Sexual health	Sexual health	(omitted)	(omitted)
Sexual safety	Sexual safety	(omitted)	(omitted)
Sexual agency	(omitted)	(omitted)	(omitted)
Becoming sexually active	Becoming sexually active	(combined with sexual decision-making)	(combined with sexual decision-making)
Relationships	Relationships	(omitted)	(omitted)
Sexual desire	Sexual desire	(omitted)	(omitted)
Puberty	Puberty	(combined with their bodies)	(combined with their bodies)
(absent)	Sexual orientation	(omitted)	(omitted)

As a second example of this more involved type of revision process, our discussions led to a modification in topics surrounding sexual identity. Members of the collaborative pointed out several limitations related to asking about lesbian, gay, bisexual, and transgender identities as one "catch-all" for non-heterosexual and non-gender conforming identities. The CAB felt that conflating sexual and gender identities served to silence the experiences of transgender individuals. To this point, the CAB recommended that, in the first revision, two separate questions be asked: one directed toward same-sex and bisexual identities, and one directed toward gender identities. Through further discussion with the CAB, we realized that even this revision might conflate gender roles with transgender identities. Thus, a second revision resulted in four discreet topics around gender and sexual identities and roles: same-sex sexuality and bisexuality, heterosexuality, transgender identity, and gender roles (masculine and feminine).

Other changes recommended by the CAB can be seen in Table 1, and included removing topics (such as sexual desire and sexual agency) and combining other topics. Some of these decisions were made for practical reasons, such as the overall length of the survey, but others were made based on likely in/accessibility of certain words, phrases, or concepts to a diverse population of parents. This iterative process took approximately six months, and resulted in a list of topics that was both responsive to the needs of community advocates, parents, and educators as well as one that could potentially fill the gaps in the research literature. The final version of the survey consisted of a series of questions regarding eighteen topics of knowledge representing inclusive and comprehensive sexuality education.

For each of these topics, we asked parents to tell us, (1) about how important it was for young people to have knowledge of that topic; (2) the grade at which they felt young people were ready to discuss that information; and (3) who they felt bore responsibility for educating young people about these domains of sexual knowledge (see Table 2 for a complete list of the survey questions). As with the specific topics, discussions within the CAB helped to determine the best format and response scale for each of these questions.

Table 2: Overview of survey items and response scales

Question Stems		Response Scales
General Items		
	What is the gender of your oldest child under the age of 18?	Female Male Transgender
	How comfortable would you be with your child's school adopting "comprehensive sexuality education" curriculum?	Very Uncomfortable Uncomfortable Equally Comfortable and Uncomfortable Comfortable Very Comfortable I don't know
	How comfortable would you be with your child's school adopting "abstinence only until marriage sexuality education" curriculum?	Very Uncomfortable Uncomfortable Equally Comfortable and Uncomfortable Comfortable Very Comfortable I don't know
	To your knowledge, what form of sexuality education curriculum is used at your child's school?	None Abstinence Only Until Marriage Abstinence Plus Comprehensive Sexuality I don't know
Items Regarding the 18-Topics (see Table 1)		

	How important do you think it is for young people to have complete knowledge about each of the topics below?	Very Unimportant
Unimportant
Neither Important nor Unimportant
Important
Very Important
I don't know
	Thinking about your oldest child under the age of 18, at what grade (or age) do you think your child was/will be first ready to discuss the following topics?	5th or before (ages 11 and younger)
6th (ages 11 - 12)
7th (ages 12 – 13)
8th (ages 13 - 14)
9th (ages 14 - 15)
10th (ages 15 - 16)
11th (ages 16 - 17)
12th (ages 17 - 18)
Adulthood (ages 19+)
	How comfortable were you or do you think you will be in discussing each of the following topics with this child at the appropriate time?	Very Uncomfortable
Uncomfortable
Equally Comfortable and Uncomfortable
Comfortable
Very Comfortable
I don't know
	Who do you think should educate young people about each topic? Mark all that apply. If you don't think any of these person or groups should educate teens about the topic, mark the last column of the row.	Parents/Guardians
Health or Sexuality Education Teachers
Other Teachers and School Staff (e.g., Nurse, Coach, Counselor, Social Worker)
Religious and/or Faith Leaders
Family Health Care Providers/Doctor's Office Personnel
None of these people should educate teens about this topic.

Note: The survey also included other questions about safe schools practices that are not reported in this paper.

In an attempt to identify a representative sample of parents from Illinois, we subsequently contracted with an independent research firm that maintained a survey research panel that included parents from across the state of Illinois. That firm recruited participants from their panel who met the following eligibility requirements: Illinois resident, aged 18 or older, parent of a middle or high school aged child. Through this process, we were able to recruit 301 participants who met all eligibility criteria. Those parents took our survey through a secure web-based interface and were compensated by the research firm for sharing their opinions.

Participants ranged in age from 25 to 75 years old ($M = 44.09$, $SD = 8.33$). Parents were mostly mothers, with 71.3% identifying as female and 28.7% as male; two further identified themselves as transgender through a separate question. The sample demonstrated a modest degree of diversity in race/ethnicity, household income, educational attainment, religion, and sexual orientation. This sample's demographics are similar to current numbers available for the state of Illinois (see Table 3 for details). Finally, several of the questions included in the survey asked participants to focus on their "oldest child under the age of 18" when responding. With regard to these focal children, parents reported 46.5% were female and 53.5% were male; no parents reported that their child was transgender. These children's ages ranged from 11 to 17 years old ($M = 15.20$, $SD = 1.47$). Although analyses of parent attitudes by these various demographics are beyond the scope of this paper, interested readers will find these results reported in Peter, Tasker, and Horn (in preparation).

Table 3: Sample demographics compared to Illinois

Demographic	Sample Percentages	Illinois Percentages
Gender[1]		
Female	71.3%	51.0%
Male	28.7%	49.0%
Transgender	0.7%	Not Reported
Race/Ethnicity[1]		
White (Non-Hispanic)	73.8%	63.7%
Latino/Hispanic	10.7%	15.8%
Black	13.3%	14.3%
Asian	0.4%	4.5%
American Indian/Alaska Native	0.4%	0.1%
Biracial/Multiracial/Other	1.3%	1.4%
Household Income[1]		
≤$39,999	25.2%	
$40,000-59,999	23.3%	Median: $56,576
$60,000-99,999	29.6%	
≥$100,000	11.0%	

Education[1]		
Attended or graduated high school	18.3%	35.1%
Some college	33.6%	21.1%
Completed college	34.6%	26.4%
Advanced degree	9.3%	11.6%
Rurality[1]		
Urban	61.1%	49.6%
Suburban	31.1%	38.2%
Rural	7.8%	12.2%
Sexual Orientation[2]		
Heterosexual	93.7%	96.2%
Sexual minority	6.3%	3.8%
Religion[3]		
Protestant	46.6%	46%
Catholic	33.6%	29%
Jewish	2.7%	1%
Muslim	1.0%	1%
Other	4.0%	3%
Atheist/Agnostic	11.6%	15%[4]

Note: 1. Illinois statistics from United States Census Bureau; 2. Illinois estimated statistic from Gates; 3. Illinois estimated statistics from Kosmin, Mayer, and Keysar; 4. The estimated category for Illinois was "no religion."

While we feel that the sample is representative of parents in communities from around the state of Illinois, we also recognize that administering the survey through this method required participants' access to a computer, and the requisite technological literacy to participate in a web-based survey. This likely impacted the overall breadth of our sample, as well as perhaps particular types of diversity within the sample, such as socioeconomic status or geographic region. In addition, since the survey was only given in English, participants had to have sufficient English-language competency to participate, which limited the linguistic diversity of our sample to English speakers.

What Parents Shared with Us

We are currently in the data interpretation phase of this project. Together, the various members of the collaborative are examining the results of the survey in an effort to co-create an understanding of what these results mean, including their implications for policy and practice and the sexual literacies of young people. In addition, our group has been focused on how we can use what we have learned from this project for multiple purposes, such as to inform advocacy and policy work, to develop educational materials for schools, parents, and communities, and to inform future research in this area. Some of the themes we have discovered are discussed further below.

Similar to other research on parents' attitudes about sexuality education, a consistent majority of parents (across demographic variables) told us that knowledge about all of the eighteen topics was important (between 55.2 and 92.5%, depending on topic) for young people. However, they rated knowledge within particular domains with varying importance (see Table 4). More specifically, parents rated knowledges within the domain of physical health and wellness as most important, followed by information about relationships, then information about sexual and gender identity, with topics in the domain of sexual pleasure being least important. Further, also confirming other research in this area, parents feel young people are ready to receive information and education about these topics predominantly in middle school. Between 50.8% and 89.0 % of the sample overall said that young people would be ready to talk about all but two issues by 8th grade. For those two issues, marriage and pleasure, a majority of parents felt that young people were ready to discuss them before or during 9th grade (61.1% and 71.4%, respectively).

Table 4: Percentage endorsement of sexual literacy topics as important for young people

Sexuality Education Topic	Percent Parents Rating "Important" or "Very Important"
Physical Health and Wellness	
Their bodies (puberty and pubertal changes)	92.30%
Pregnancy	92.20%
Sexually transmitted diseases and infections	91.50%
Dating violence	90.20%
Sexual protection (contraception and birth control)	88.50%
Parenting	87.40%
Sexual decision-kaing such as when to become sexually active	87.20%
Abstaining from sexual activity	84.00%
Abortion	77.80%
Relationships	
Dating	86.90%
Marriage	81.00%
Romantic love	78.00%
Sexual and Gender Identity	
Heterosexuality	80.60%
Same-sex sexuality and bisexuality	68.20%

Gender roles (masculine and feminine)	66.20%
Transgender identity	59.10%
Pleasure	
Masturbation	57.00%
Sexual pleasure	55.20%

When asked about who, if anyone, should be responsible for discussing these sexual knowledge topics with young people, a majority of parents said they were primarily responsible for educating their adolescent child about these topics. Interestingly, almost all parents felt responsible for providing information about topics related to physical health and wellness (90.4-95.3%) and relationships (94.7-95.0%), with slightly fewer parents saying they were responsible for topics related to sexual and gender identity (85.0-90.0%) and pleasure (81.1-81.1%). Parents often did not view themselves as solely responsible for sexuality education, however. In fact, a majority of parents who viewed themselves as responsible for discussing topics in the domains of physical health and identity endorsed sharing these responsibilities with other community members. Further, a large minority of parents who viewed themselves as responsible for topics relating to relationships and pleasure endorsed sharing these responsibilities with other community members. Parents most often identified sexuality education teachers as sharing the responsibility for topics within physical health and wellness (43.3-70.2%) and identity (44.2-51.6%), and less often for pleasure (34.0-39.8%) or relationships (21.3-28.3%). Few parents endorsed the involvement of other school staff, religious or faith leaders, or doctors as sharing responsibility for these topics.

It is worth noting that a small minority of parents did not view themselves as responsible for sexuality education. Of the parents who did not identify themselves as responsible, many felt that sexuality education teachers, but very rarely other groups, were responsible for covering identity (42.2-51.2%), some aspects of physical health and wellness (14.3-75.0%), relationships (31.3-66.7%), and a minority wanted topics of pleasure discussed (29.8-35.1%).

Conclusion and Implications

The conclusions and implications we draw from this work are fourfold. The first two relate to our specific findings regarding parental attitudes about the role that schools and community members should play in helping young people develop their sexual literacy. The last two of these conclusions and implications relate to the process and benefits achieved through the ongoing and collaborative nature of this university-community partnership. Not only will this collaborative process guide our future efforts on Project Safe SPACES, but it can also serve as a template for other researchers and community members who may be seeking to develop collaborative, mutually beneficial projects.

With regard to the specific findings of our survey, a clear majority of Illinois parents who shared their beliefs with us viewed knowledge about all eighteen sexuality topics as important, and also as mostly appropriate for young people to know before they leave middle school. In fact, many parents indicated that some sexual literacy conversations should begin as early as elementary school, but certainly before high school. Parents also overwhelmingly endorsed bearing some responsibility themselves for educating young people about sexuality and sexual health. Importantly, many parents also supported a clear role for other members of the community in helping young people develop sexual literacy. In particular, parents viewed this responsibility as being shared with sexuality and sexual health educators in schools. Taken together, these results demonstrate that parents endorsed youth's access to the same diversity of sexual and relational literacies that has been supported by research and advocated for by groups focused on fostering healthy sexuality and sexual decision-making by young people. Notably, these findings challenge assumptions that parents are key barriers to a more comprehensive sexuality curriculum, and show us, instead, that they may more accurately be perceived as not just supporters and potential advocates, but also as critical stakeholders in the developing sexual literacies of their children. In fact, parents' awareness of the physical changes in very young children, as well as young children's questions about their own bodies, their families, and different types of social relationships may prompt parents to begin to help children in developing sexual literacies in very early childhood before they even enter the realm of schooling.

As such, parents should be recognized as the first sexuality educators that young people encounter. These findings have implications for expanding sexuality education in two important ways. First and foremost, our findings suggest that parents want sexuality education curriculum included in earlier grades, and, in particular, during the middle school years. Second, efforts to improve young people's sexual literacies can be enhanced by moving from a deficit- and risk-based model of sexuality education to one that views sexuality, sexual health, and sexual rights as a positive and critical part of development. Our work makes evident that the primary barrier to expanding sexuality education is not likely to be the beliefs of parents overall, but may, in fact, be the voices of a vocal minority of parents who oppose these curricula and/or the unquestioned fears of administrators and policy makers.

With regard to the implications of the specific processes of inquiry that have guided us, this work further highlights the importance of questioning the assumptions one brings into her or his work, and the necessity of seeking out the voices of those who are not already being heard (Langhout and Thomas; Rappaport). Through collaborative interpretation with the CAB, we identified the need to make our research findings accessible to schools, parents, and communities. To that end, the CAB, with the help of communications professionals, has begun to develop a series of research briefs aimed at communicating to parents that they are not alone in their beliefs that young people should be exposed to a diverse array of topics regarding sexuality. The research briefs are also intended to communicate to school leaders, teachers, counselors, and other educators that parents support the inclusion of information about diverse sexual identities and comprehensive sexuality education topics in school, as well as to communicate to young people that their sexual health and sexual rights matter. To view and/or download the first completed brief in the series, please go to the following link: http://education.uic.edu/773-safespaces.

This broad dissemination of our findings may contribute to better mutual understanding by all involved, negating negative stereotypes about parental attitudes and truly allowing us, as a broader community, to consider sexual health education a community literacy activity. The awareness that many fellow parents are in favor of comprehensive and inclusive curricula may serve to empower this often-unheard majority of parents to become allies and advocates around these issues. In keeping with the overall vision for our project, it is our hope that the research findings will serve as a catalyst for parents, educators, and young people themselves to work toward schools becoming places "*in which people talk about gender, sex, and sexuality and grapple with the complexity of these issues in structured (traditional), non-structured, supported, developmentally appropriate, and safe ways.*" It is also our hope that this work, as well as related and ongoing projects, will aid in achieving the goal that all young people – regardless of sexual orientation, gender identity, relationships status, or pregnancy or parenting status – are able to learn about sexuality and sexual health in environments free from harassment, discrimination, ridicule, and shame.

Moreover, our previous discussion of CAB input into the survey's content and design helps to highlight some of the unique features and benefits of our university-community collaboration. For instance, through the collaborative process, other members of the CAB helped the research team to separate out the concepts of sexual identity and gender identity, and, consequently, to ask about them as two distinct items. As a result, we discovered through the survey that parents' views actually differed on these two topics. This is a differentiation we would not have understood had it not been for the collective conversations of the CAB in helping to ensure that the survey was relevant and legible across communities.

Finally, this project constitutes only one part of an ongoing relationship between the various partners within the Safe SPACES collaborative. In moving forward, we will continue to use the strengths of our collaboration to develop studies and advocacy activities that make legible our research findings for a variety of stakeholders throughout the state, further engaging Illinois parents in conversation and using the results for effective community advocacy. To date, not only has the CAB employed strategic communication by utilizing better survey measures to address parents, it has also continued to work to uncover the varied meanings that the research results have for different constituencies. (For an example of this, see the research brief described above).

In essence, through being a part of CAB, those of us who are members of the research team were pushed to become community literacy workers. Moreover, our assumptions as researchers, educators, and youth advocates were transformed, evolving from viewing parents as only gatekeepers to expanding the sexuality narratives allowed in schools to viewing parents as critical partners in the development of sexual literacies for all young people. It is our hope that our continued collaborative work will ensure that the voices of all parents become a critical thread in the ongoing narrative regarding the sexual literacies of young people. We also expect that parents will continue to be positioned as, and further empowered to be, community literacy workers. In this way, parents will continue to be in partnership with their children and other adult allies to facilitate making sexual knowledges legible within all of the communities in which young people live, learn, and grow.

Acknowledgments

Correspondence concerning this article should be send to Stacey S. Horn, Ph.D. at sshorn@uic.edu. The authors thank Drs. Adela Licona, Stephen Russell, and Leah Stauber for their helpful comments and suggestions for improving our manuscript. In addition, the authors thank the Safe SPACES team and the Community Advisory Board for their invaluable work and input on the project. The research presented here was funded in part by a grant from the Ford Foundation to Stacey Horn, Ph.D. and Shannon Sullivan, MPH. This study was approved by the UIC IRB under protocol # 2011-1092. Portions of this study have been presented at the biennial meeting of the Society for Research in Child Development in Seattle, WA on April 18, 2013 and the National Safe Schools Roundtable, Chicago, IL, November 2012.

Endnotes

1. "Sexual Health is a state of physical, emotional, mental, and social well-being in relation to sexuality; it is not merely the absence of disease, dysfunction or infirmity. Sexual health requires a positive and respectful approach to sexuality and sexual relationships, as well as the possibility of having pleasurable and safe sexual experiences, free of coercion, discrimination and violence. For sexual health to be attained and maintained, the sexual rights of all persons must be respected, protected and fulfilled. Sexual Rights embrace human rights that are already recognized in national laws, international human rights documents and other consensus statements. They include the right of all persons, free of coercion, discrimination and violence, to: The highest attainable standard of sexual health, including access to sexual and reproductive health care services; Seek, receive and impart information related to sexuality; Sexuality education; Respect for bodily integrity; Choose their partner; Decide to be sexually active or not; Consensual sexual relations; Consensual marriage; Decide whether or not, and when, to have children; and Pursue a satisfying, safe and pleasurable sex life." (retrieved from: http://www.who.int/reproductivehealth/topics/gender_rights/sexual_health/en/)

Works Cited

Allen, Louisa. "'They Think You Shouldn't Be Having Sex Anyway': Young People's Suggestions for Improving Sexuality Education Content." *Sexualities* 11.5 (2008): 573-594. Print.

____. "Closing Sex Education's Knowledge/Practice Gap: The Reconceptualisation of Young people's Sexual Knowledge." *Sex Education* 2 (2001): 109-122. Print.

Alexander, Sharon J. and Stephen R. Jorgensen. "Sex Education for Early Adolescents: A Study of Parents and Students." *The Journal of Early Adolescence* 3.4 (1983): 315-325. Print.

Brooks-Gunn, Jeanne and Julia A. Graber. "What's sex got to do with it? The development of sexual identities during adolescence." *Rutgers Series on Self and Social Identity* 2 (1999): 155-184. Print.

Byers, E. Sandra, Heather A. Sears, and Angela D. Weaver. "Parents' Reports of Sexual Communication with Children in Kindergarten to Grade 8." *Journal of Marriage and Family* 70.1 (2008): 86-96. Print.

Catalog for Federal Domestic Assistance. *Community-based abstinence education (CBAE).* No. 93.010, Department of Health and Human Services, Administration for Children and Families. Web.

Constantine, Norman A., Petra Jerman, and Alice X. Huang. "California Parents' Preferences and Beliefs Regarding School-Based Sex Education Policy." *Perspectives on Sexual and Reproductive Health* 39.3 (2007): 167-175. Print.

Eisenberg, Marla, Nikki Madsen, Jennifer A. Oliphant, and Michael Resnick."Policies, Principals and Parents: Multilevel Challenges and Supports in Teaching Sexuality Education." *Sex Education* 12.3 (2012): 317-329. Print.

Gates, Gary J. *Same-sex Couples and the Gay, Lesbian, Bisexual Population: New Estimates from the American Community Survey.* Los Angeles: The Williams Institute on Sexual Orientation Law and Public Policy, 2006. Print.

Institute of Medicine of the National Academies. "No Time to Lose: Getting More from HIV Prevention." National Academy Press, 2001. Print and PDF file.

Jaccard, James, Patricia J. Dittus, and Vivian V. Gordon. "Maternal correlates of adolescent sexual and contraceptive behavior." *Family Planning Perspectives* 28.4 (1996): 159-165 +185. Print.

Jorgensen, Stephen R., and Sharon J. Alexander. "Research on adolescent pregnancy-risk: Implications for sex education programs." *Theory into Practice* 22.2 (1983): 125-133. Print.

Kirby, Douglas B. "The Impact of Abstinence and Comprehensive Sex and STD/HIV Education Programs on Adolescent Sexual Behavior." *Sexuality Research & Social Policy: A Journal of the NSRC* 5.3 (2008): 18-27. Web.

Kosmin, Barry A., Egon Mayer, and Ariela Keysar. "American Religious Identification Survey." New York: The Graduate Center of the City University of New York, 2001: 40. PDF file.

Lagus, Kathryn A., Debra H. Bernat, Linda H. Bearinger, Michael D. Resnick, and Marla E. Eisenberg. "Parental Perspectives on Sources of Sex Information for Young People." *Journal of Adolescent Health* 49.1 (2011): 87-89. Print.

Landry, David J., Lisa Kaeser, and Cory L. Richards. "Abstinence promotion and the provision of information about contraception in public school district sexuality education policies." *Family Planning Perspectives* 31.6 (1999): 280-286. Print.

Langhout, Regina Day, and Elizabeth Thomas. "Imagining participatory action research in collaboration with children: An introduction." *American Journal of Community Psychology* 46.1 (2010): 60-66. Print.

Martin, Carol Lynn, and Diane N. Ruble. "Patterns of Gender Development." *Annual Review of Psychology* 61 (2010): 353-381. Print.

National Guidelines Taskforce. "Guidelines for Comprehensive Sexuality Education (3rd edition): Kindergarten through 12th grade." Sexuality Information and Education Council of the United States, 2004. PDF file.

Rappaport, Julian. "Community narratives: Tales of terror and joy." *American Journal of Community Psychology* 28.1 (2000): 1-24. Print.

Secor-Turner, Molly, Renee E. Seaving, Marla E. Eisenberg and Carol Skay. "Associations between Sexually Experienced Adolescents' Sources of Information about Sex and Sexual Risk Outcomes." *Sex Education* 11.4 (2011): 489-500. Print.

Society for Adolescent Medicine. "Reproductive Health Care for Adolescents: Position Paper." *Journal of Adolescent Health* 12 (1991): 649-661. Print.

Solomon-Fears, Carmen. "Teenage Pregnancy Prevention: Statistics and Programs." Congressional Research Service. Report No. RS20301. 2013. Web. 14 July 2013.

Somers, Cheryl L., and Amy T. Surmann. "Adolescents' Preferences for Source of Sex Education." *Child Study Journal* 34.1 (2004): 47-59. Print.

United States Census Bureau. *State and County Quick Facts*. Web. 6 June 2013.

Stacey S. Horn, Ph.D., Associate Professor, Department of Educational Psychology, University of Illinois-Chicago (sshorn@uic.edu); Christina R. Peter, MA, University of Illinois-Chicago (cpeter34@uic.edu); Timothy B. Tasker, doctoral student, University of Illinois-Chicago (ttaske2@uic.edu); Shannon L. Sullivan, MPH, Executive Director, Illinois Safe Schools Alliance (shannon@illinoissafeschools.org).

Poetry

Public Speaking
Niki Herd

You want to know why there aren't
more cute girls in speech class

and I feel like I should offer a history
lesson on the objectification of women, or

suggest more attention be paid
to your grades, which are miserably sore.

Instead, I'm reminded of the boy
from this morning's commute

how he model-walked his freedom
down that thread of a bus aisle

in his bright purples and pinks, and who
like you girl, is confident in youth

and a young sexuality in a world
hesitantly unraveling itself towards

progress while still clinging to the easy
pronunciation of words like:

bull-dagger, faggot, sissy and dyke.

A world never safe when one brick
inches itself away, how the rest

of the wall fears more will follow
and the institution come tumbling down.

Next week you will visit again, this

time with a pretty girl on your arm
and while the office workers avert

their eyes to this unsealed romance

we will talk class and grades and plans

for spring break. And as you leave
the office with your hand in unison

with the hand of the woman you're with
you will never hear the words lurking

silent behind averted eyes.
You will never get to see my ever so

discreet, but proud smile, tight like
some kind of fist raised in the air.

Man
Zack Taylor

Mom,
Just 17 laying in a hospital bed
Cradling me
What kind of man did you hope I would be?

Creating illusions
plans
presumptions
Your premeditated predictions
dream and fantasize the man wanted out of me
I'm seventeen years old
trying to figure out what "man" means.
Society got me twisted
deadbeats to heartthrobs
drug dealers and political leaders
overly famous sports men to businessmen in suits

Mom,
What kind of stereotype of a man did you want me to be?

I never thought you'd want me to be
immoral
useless
philandering
A man using sugar coated kisses
treating women like bitches
Squandering for cash in empty pockets
Pockets empty
Checks flying away
Like my dignity
Supporting unforgiving ex-wives
fatherless children
Suspected you wanted a
ladies man
out of me

I believed dad was the perfect man
I could be
Owning mistakes
like pastors own beliefs
Taking responsibilities
instead of taking risks

Giving up teenage years
like alcoholics give up liquor
Is that the kind of man you expect me to be?
Mom,
I can't be
I'm not the type to raise a family at 17.

Image your first born
a homo.
Fathoming that your son would kiss boys
play with girl toys
trade in pregnancies for adoption agencies
fighting
for the right of equal marriage opportunities
Was that ever the kind of man you dreamt I would be?
Overhearing
you fear what life is going to be
unaccepting school kids
who use cruel games,
gain power over sexual minorities.
If ever being put down as a fag
queer
homosexual being
I would have the strength
to stand on my own two feet
keep my composure
because motherly arms taught me how to do so.
Isn't that the kind of man you wanted me to be.

Mom
How do you even define a man?

Dictionaries say
"Man" an adult who has opposite
characteristics of a woman
Definition two said
"generic use of the word referring to human beings"
example: "it is every man for himself"
Suggested that a male person has to "play significant role in the life
(as in a husband or a boyfriend or a lover)
of a particular-
-*woman.*"

Not needing shallow Webster's or dictionaries with hollow meanings
Telling me what a man is

Mother taught me how to respect
not only women
but human beings

If definition of "man" is male
who loves a human
Yes mom
I am a man

I love you dearly.

Boom

Sammy Dominguez and Zack Taylor

Shotguns sound from the throats of classmates,
"freak"
"dyke"

Slurs,
slung like hammers
demolishing any self-pride
I had mustered up
just to show
my face
at school today.

"Fucking faggot."

I duck into a bathroom stall
waiting for the halls to clear
finally reach my desk
as I mend
my wounds
from their words.

my state of mind
is anything
but healed.

I'm thinking… today cold steel could ease my pain.

The jokes were never ending.
I stopped feeling safe.
Today.
they keyed "lesbian" into my car.

Today.
they spat in my face
told me to
wipe off my mascara.

Today.
I found death threats
in my notebook.

Today.

I found out
I can fit in a locker.

What do you do with a box of bullets when you only need one?

Raped.
They think they can fix me.

Beaten down
every time
I walk home.

I can't even really go home.
The door is never open for me.
My mother always wanted a princess,
All she sees in me,
is a dragon.

I was never the popular jock
my father wanted.
When he looks at me
he thinks "faggot."

So why leave a note, when nobody ever cared?

It's not like I had any true friends.
Harassment helps 28% of LGBT teens give up on education
Nobody cares about who I am.
Teachers ignore homophobic insults 97% of the time.
Maybe I deserved every dirty slur.
LGBTQ youth are 4-5 times more likely to experience severe depression.

The weight in my hand is nothing compared to the weight in my chest.

There is no place for me, this world doesn't want me.
1 in 4 homeless youth identify as LGBTQ. who come out of the closet get tossed onto the street
Maybe I should just leave.
LGBTQ teens are 2-3 times more likely to commit suicide than their straight peers.
I hate everything I am.
3 LGBTQ teens commit suicide every day.

Billy Lucas, age 15
Asher Brown, age 13
Cody Barker, age 17
Chloe Lacey, age 19

Tyler Clementi, age 18
Samantha Johnson, age 13
Aiyisha Hassan, age 19
Harrison Brown, age 15
Seth Welsh, age 13
Raymond Chase, age 19
Brandon Elizares, age 16
Phillip Parker, age 14
Zach Harrington, age 19
Jamey Rodemeyer, age 14
Jack Reese, age 17

Nothing is more inviting now than shiny steel shaking as it sets against my temple.

I don't understand why I was born a fuck-up
Why it had to be me that no one would love
Why the only thing that shined in my life,
Was a hand gun.

So.
Boom.
That's it.

fall 2013

Project Connect Zine

INTRO

Youth Activists from: Chicago • Detroit • San Francisco • Tucson

shared knowledge + their work around...

YOUTH • RIGHTS • SEXUALITY

with each other in Fall 2012 / Spring 2013. They collectively created this ZINE to:

- **show** solidarity.
- **inspire** long term activism.
- **build** community.

¡Muchas Gracias a Todxs!

- Alliance Youth Committee, Chicago, IL
  Illinois Safe Schools Alliance
  Project Safe Spaces
  University of Illinois at Chicago

- Detroit Hispanic Development Corporation, Detroit MI
  Alternatives for Girls
  Ruth Ellis Center
  Detroit Youth Passages
  Florida International University
  University of Michigan

- ELAYO, Youth Advisory Group, San Francisco CA
  Empower Latino Youth
  California Latinas for Reproductive Justice
  Health Equity Institute
  San Francisco State University

- Tucson Youth Poetry Slam, Tucson AZ
  Crossroads Collaborative
  University of Arizona
  Spoken Futures, INC

Sarah Gonzales	Stacey Sullivan	Stacey Horn
TruthSarita, LLC	Illinois Safe Schools	University of Illinois at Chicago

FORDFOUNDATION

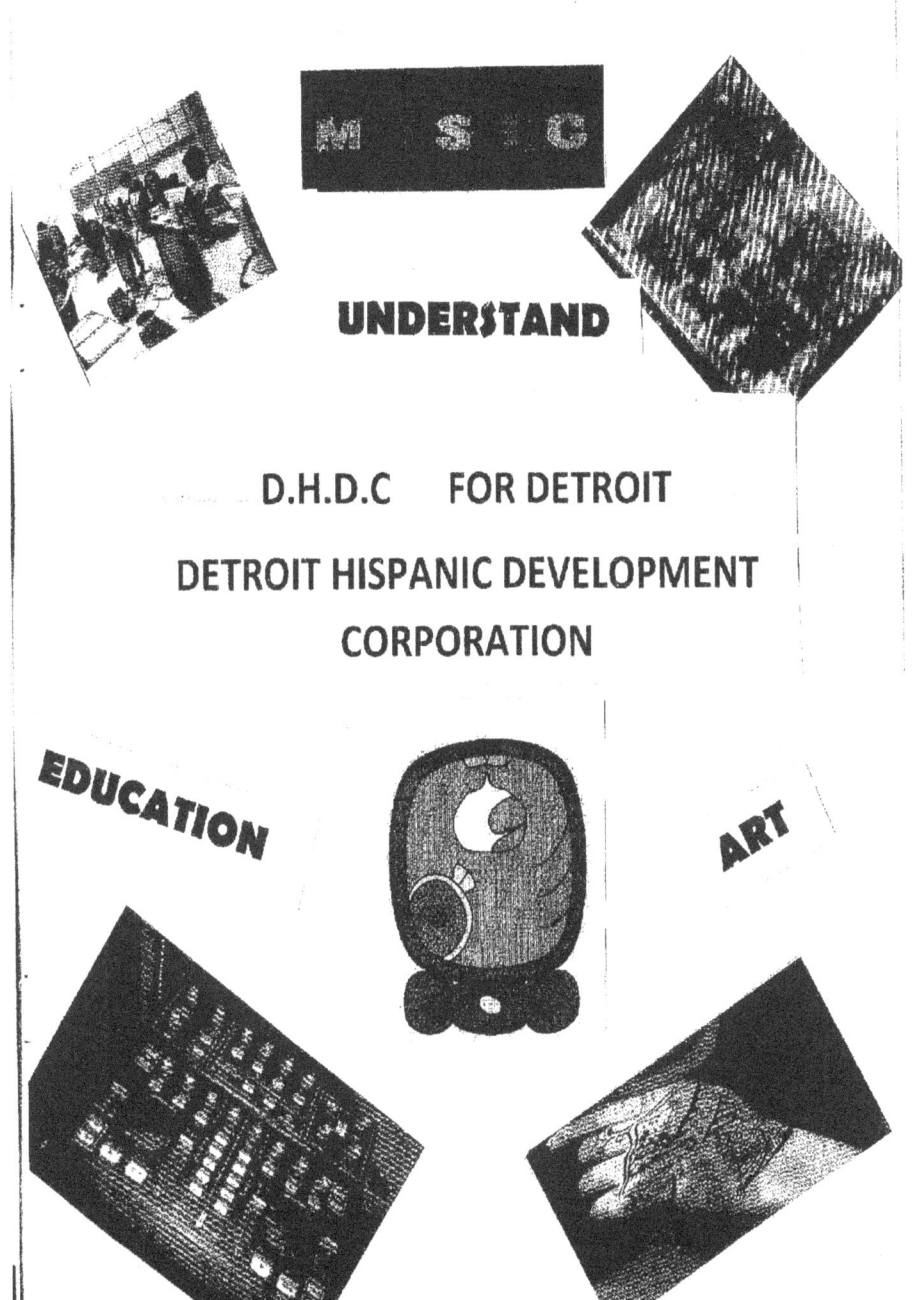

CHANGE   Power

Revolution   STRENGTH

Unity

Family

DARE

Freedom   Honor

Detroit Youth Passages

• Detroit Hispanic Development Corp

• Alternative for Girls

• Ruth Ellis

Love

fall 2013

We are individuals coming
together as a community
to change perspectives, create
assets, & support each other towards
success. We search for a positive
outlook within each other while
looking towards strength in our
communities in order
to change & break
stereotypes. The
different pathways
& diversity we
bring forth, allow us
to open & expand
our minds.

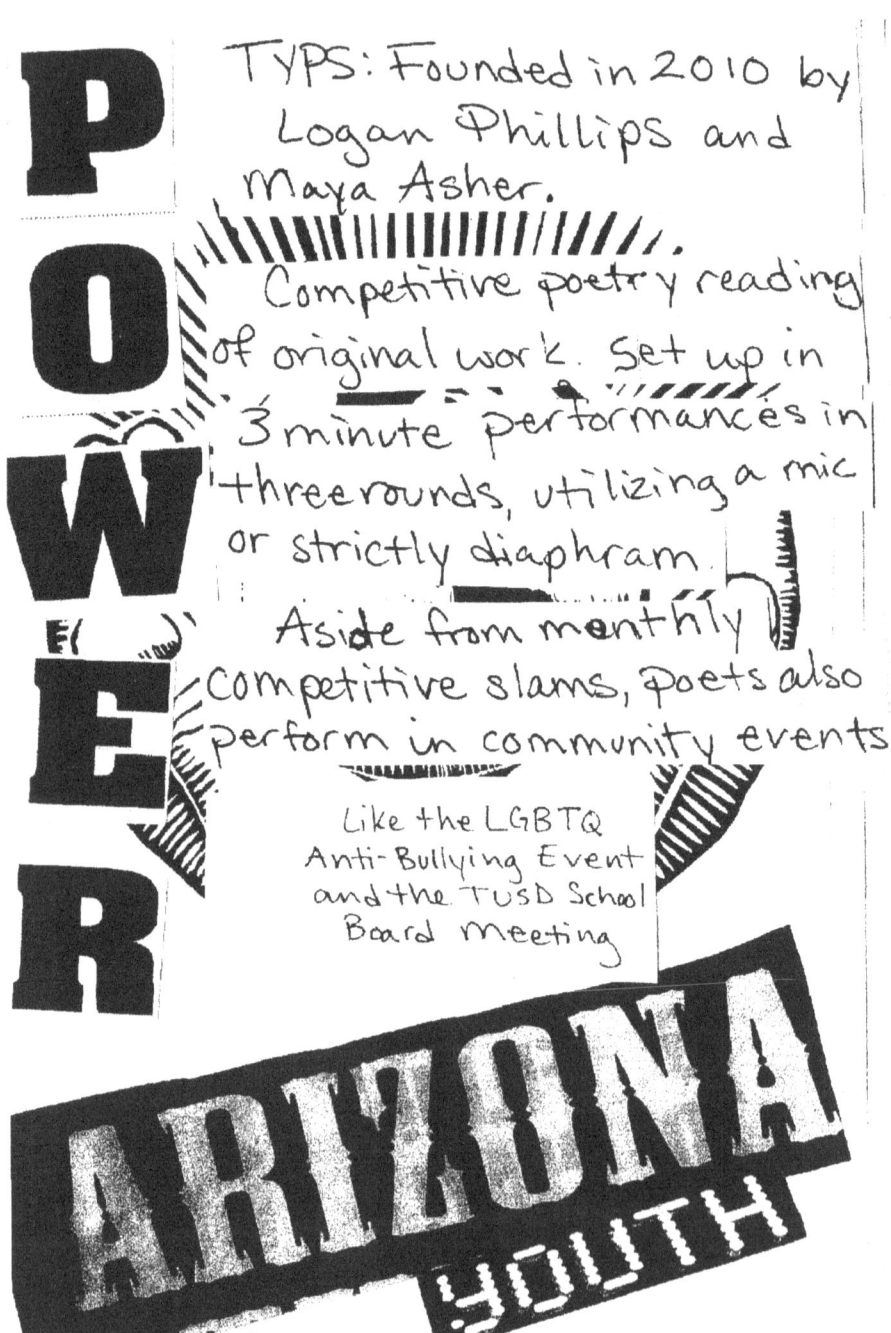

community literacy journal

J. Sarah Gonzales believes the intersection of art and activism is a critical place for community survival. After years of working for Universities and non-profits doing community work and youth organizing on racial justice in Arizona, she founded her own national social justice consulting company, TruthSarita, LLC which supports building collective power to dismantle inequity. Sarah also serves as Codirector of Spoken Futures, Inc. developing programs including Tucson Youth Poetry Slam and Liberation Lyrics, which create spaces for youth to process and address issues such as the school to prison pipeline, LGBTQ rights and migrant justice through spoken word poetry. In addition to facilitation, training and youth organizing work, Sarah is an extensive haiku writer, fierce dance floor occupier and a trickster performance artist whose recent work landed her in 6th place in the Arizona US Presidential Primaries in 2012. She can be reached at sarah@truthsarita.com.

Book and New Media Reviews

Slam School: Learning Through Conflict in the Hip-Hop and Spoken Word Classroom
Bronwen E. Low
Stanford University Press, 2011. 208 pp.
ISBN: 9780804763660 $21.95

Reviewed by Amanda Fields
University of Arizona

In *Slam School: Learning Through Conflict in the Hip-Hop and Spoken Word Classroom*, Bronwen E. Low argues for the significance of critical hip-hop pedagogies, particularly when engaging with racial and social conflicts in educational settings. Low collaborated with a teacher at an urban arts magnet high school in the northeastern United States through a performance poetry course that was taught using a hip-hop and spoken word curriculum. Overall, Low's book is useful for community literacy scholars as an application and assessment of a popular practice and growing pedagogy in schools and community organizations.

Low collected data, including audiovisual recordings, for two years. She transcribed and coded recordings through the use of grounded theory as described by Strauss and Corbin (1990); for instance, initial coding of broad themes such as race transitioned to more specific codes as the transcriptions offered particular data for Low to identify and interpret. The more general themes were altered, then, once Low discovered that conflict was central to the learning experience in a hip-hop and spoken word classroom. Classroom conflicts ranged from issues of race, ethnicity, and gender to generational distinctions and understandings of hip-hop; the terminology Low used to define and code conflict included "(mis)understanding," "offense," "mistranslation," and "difference" (Low xii).

Low argues for more direct engagement with cultural differences in a context where classrooms are increasingly diverse in terms of ethnic backgrounds, while most of the teachers remain white. This context is of particular interest to Low because of the opportunity for knowledge-making that can come from cultural conflicts bound to arise in a hip-hop and spoken word curriculum. Low's experiences with hip-hop and spoken word were primarily on a theoretical level, while the high school teacher had had little experience with these genres in either theory or practice. However, Low and her partner teacher made it a point to avoid the view that, because they did not have tangible experience with hip-hop and spoken word, they should not be involved in developing such a curriculum and pedagogy alongside students. Extant hip-hop pedagogy assumes the instructor's intricate knowledge of the culture, but Low claims that the story told in this book—wherein a teacher who is unfamiliar with hip-hop culture nonetheless integrates it into the classroom as part of an exchanged learning experience alongside students—is a more likely scenario based on the current demographics of many classrooms. Indeed, Low identifies "the dynamics of cultural insider and outsider-ness in teaching" as one of the book's main concerns (3).

According to Low, some conflicts arise when hip-hop is introduced into classroom settings because much hip-hop discourse is critical of traditional approaches in education; thus, it can be difficult to convince administrators of the value of a hip-hop curriculum. Low argues that a pedagogy of the complexity of hip-hop culture, in terms of the politics surrounding issues such as "gender, violence, sexuality, materialism, race, and language," is crucial to curricula, in spite of the potential resistance of administrators in incorporating these subjects into the curriculum (1). At the same time, spoken word and slam poetry, themselves outgrowths of hip-hop, are seen as more inclusive for a diverse population of students than rap, which is "marked as black." Low claims that there have been well-known slam poets, on the other hand, from "all cultural groups" (14). The performance poetry course detailed in this book exists within this framework and with these assumptions, so that Low forwards a "trans-disciplinary critical hip-hop pedagogy" that "explores racism in intersection with other modes of oppression and is centered on the experiences and knowledge of students of color" (20).

The book is organized around the following subjects: Low gives a historical overview of hip-hop, spoken word, and slam poetry, in addition to a summary of her methods and purpose (Chapter 1). Low also discusses the idea of "keeping it real" as a theoretical framework and considers how students interpreted and learned about the concept of "authenticity" (Chapter 2). She considers how to foster critical detachment in relationship to the issue of authenticity and its significance to youth. She then argues for a pedagogy that values conflict as well as awareness of multiple interpretations as conflict unfolds (Chapter 3). These pedagogical queries are used as a way to analyze how discussions about hip-hop, students' production of poetry, and identities, as well as specific interactions within the class, may have been influenced by the subject of race (Chapter 4). Discourses of race connect with an examination of the language of hip-hop and controversies surrounding language, such as the prominent use of "bitches" and "ho's" in rap (Chapter 5). Low rounds out the book with a general discussion of how hip-hop curricula are spreading, while arguing for greater communication among schools and community organizations regarding how such pedagogies can be shared (Chapter 6). Low proposes four elements to consider in hip-hop education: "(1) hip-hop education as a movement; (2) the fluorescence of hip-hop programming outside of schools; (3) the slam poetry movement taking America by storm; and (4) multilingual, multicultural, and global hip-hop," all of which "respond, in different ways, to the challenges posed by hip-hop education" (146).

Low devotes a large space in the book to the question of authenticity, or "keeping it real"; this is a significant query in terms of the development of young people and the knowledges they bring to the table that enhance and can guide educational experiences. Much of the book is focused on the pedagogy and practices that encouraged students to explore how they define and are defined by notions of authenticity. Low's analysis offers the opportunity for other scholars to more deeply consider the relationship between authenticity and the performative, in terms of forming a viable curriculum that honors personal experience and invention while fostering critical cognizance of socially constructed elements of experience and genre. As Low notes, the concept of authenticity is problematic in that performativity must be taken into account and a focus on an "authentic self" is essentialist. Yet the concept cannot be ignored in relationship to a hip-hop curriculum, as so much of hip-hop is focused on self-revelations of "truth." Low discovers that it is challenging to encourage experiential artistic production while fostering an awareness of the representational nature of such productions; in the classroom, it is difficult to determine how to fit together critical awareness with a vibrant, genuine connection with one's experiential expressions, particularly if these expressions are critiqued based on perceived authenticity.

Also of interest is the fact that Low works across disciplines (e.g., poetics, cultural studies) to build her study and argument, thus emphasizing the significance of interdisciplinary engagements—particularly in relation to the focus on conflict in the classroom. Low also works to read events from multiple interpretations, to argue "against easy analyses of what actually happened," and to look for the unknown or unexpected (26). This method encourages openness about the limitations of her perspective. It also emphasizes the opportunities and limitations in perspective offered by various constituents involved in the hip-hop curriculum—from students to teachers to parents. Low's approach, of juxtaposing multiple interpretations of an event, is one step toward focusing more intently on listening and audience. This practice is one that any discussion of conflict and pedagogy should feature, and scholars who engage with this book will have found another tool for doing so.

Slam School has several implications for community literacy studies. Its broadest implication is the possibility of bringing together work in the community and in schools through an established and complicated art form. The book offers a practical delineation of a curriculum that articulates context-specific conflicts but demonstrates broader significance for diverse community literacy contexts. Low also calls for more work between community organizations and schools, in terms of sharing and learning from these pedagogies. Finally, the book provides a working frame for cross-cultural communications and community literacies, and for interacting across cultures along with youth.

The book's exploration of conflict through a hip-hop pedagogy converses with other recent attempts to progress through and across conflicting ideas to promote and act toward social change. For instance, Linda Flower's *Community Literacy and the Rhetoric of Public Engagement* (2008) offers strategies for resolving conflict and creating active change as it draws on the lessons of a community partnership that lasted nearly a decade. In contrast to Low's work, Flower's long-term project occurred outside of the classroom, and thus might have escaped some of the intra-school hierarchies experienced by young people. Flower and Low both focus on asset-driven approaches that view young people as capable of manifesting agency for social change, but acknowledge that the circumstances that youth might recognize as exigent vary, and as such invite different remediating possibilities.

Late in *Slam School*, Low suggests that community organizations could learn from the pedagogy and curriculum developed at schools, and vice-versa. Her suggestions would interest those scholars invested in creating equitable exchanges between community organizations and schools. However, since Low's book is not focused on working with community organizations, suggestions relating to community-school partnerships seem to serve mostly as a typical way to wrap up an academic book, rather than a concrete delineation of partnership possibilities. Still, the subject of hip-hop pedagogy is a clear bridge across many contexts of community literacy studies, in particular as it makes students legible as knowledge-seekers authentically engaged in an education process that comprises culturally relevant curricula.

Amanda Fields is a Crossroads Scholar and Ph.D. candidate in Rhetoric, Composition, and the Teaching of English at the University of Arizona (afields@email.arizona.edu).

Valuing Youth Voices and Differences through Community Literacy Projects: Review of *Detroit Future Youth Curriculum Mixtape* and *Freeing Ourselves: A Guide to Health and Self-Love for Brown Bois*

Reviewed by Londie T. Martin
University of Arizona

When viewed together, the two community-based publications reviewed here—*Detroit Future Youth Curriculum Mixtape* and *Freeing Ourselves: A Guide to Health and Self Love for Brown Bois*—offer practitioners working within contexts that bridge academic and local community locations invaluable pedagogical materials and resources for imagining and practicing community literacy partnerships. These new forms of partnership complicate understandings of racialized, classed, sexualized, and gendered differences by valuing youth and working to make them legible as holders and creators of knowledge—as the experts on their own lived experiences.

In *Community Literacy and the Rhetoric of Public Engagement* (2008), Linda Flower defines community literacy as "a rhetorical practice for inquiry and social change." She asserts a vision of community engagement through which practitioners—across academic and local community contexts—work to practice ways of knowing that challenge and reimagine lived experiences of difference and inequality as they articulate with multiple ways of performing identities (Flower 221). In her work, Flower understands community literacy as

a space for practicing community (broadly defined) as "public dialogue across differences of culture, class, discourse, race, gender, and power shaped by the explicit goals of discovery and change" (261-65). Yet, I want to extend Flower's articulation of community, literacy, and difference by acknowledging that working *across* difference is sometimes less transformative than working *with* difference; in these cases, the goal is not to elide or smooth over difference, but to engage with difference as a necessary and radical component of grassroots social transformation. As Eve Kosofsky Sedgwick argues in *Epistemology of the Closet*, "People are different from each other" (22); working to recognize and understand difference as necessary and valuable should be central to the goals of radical and sustainable community literacy projects, like those reviewed here.

Conceived as a collaborative, social justice venture among youth and adult allies working with community organizations in Detroit, *Detroit Future Youth Curriculum Mixtape* is an assemblage of community-authored literacy workshops rooted in a place-based understanding of youth who encounter daily not only Detroit's social inequalities, but also the stereotypical narratives that circulate about Detroit youth and their particular urban location. Detroit Future Youth, an organization that works to build and strengthen youth coalition in Detroit, advocates multimedia literacy and production as particularly effective ways for youth and adult allies to challenge and revision the larger, deficit-driven narratives of youth—particularly youth of color—that circulate through dominant media channels. As such, the *Detroit Future Youth Curriculum Mixtape* print curriculum is accompanied by a flash drive compilation of lesson-plan resources and youth-produced media. In light of a recent report from the Pew Research Center showing that youth living in lower socioeconomic conditions are outpacing their economically wealthier counterparts in terms of mobile access to Internet and social media, it is apparent that media literacy and production hold the potential for youth-driven social change at the grassroots level (2).

Across the *Detroit Future Youth Curriculum Mixtape*, the editors identify three relational "layers of impact": "Personal impact," in which youth and adult allies take the materials offered in the curriculum and modify them within the context-specific locations of their communities; "Community impact," in which the curriculum practiced within and across communities facilitates and sustains conversation and coalition; and "Social change impact," in which youth and adult allies engage the curriculum as a way of performing a more just and equitable future within the experience of present realities (8). While detailing the 13 workshop lesson plans offered within the *Curriculum Mixtape* is beyond the scope of this review, a snapshot of the kinds of pedagogical activities offered in the collected materials illustrates their potential for use in a variety of community literacy contexts. For example, Young Nation, a grassroots youth organization in south Detroit, describes a workshop focused on identifying topics of interest to youth, connecting these topics to place-specific lived realities, and working with youth to transform or produce new spaces of youth community that reimagine the present. In another chapter, Freeing a Mind Everywhere (FAME, a youth-driven project of Vanguard Community Development Corporation) offers a workshop designed to introduce youth to blogging and vlogging as practices for sharing counterstories.

Combined with the photography workshop offered by the Urban Neighborhood Initiative's Real Media program and the creative writing exercises offered by the Detroit Asian Youth Project, the resources for interview practice and social media exploration sustained throughout the *Detroit Future Youth Curriculum Mixtape* come alive; the curriculum is an inventive resource for youth and adult allies interested in multimodal ways of crafting social-media-ready counterstories that are grounded in community-based research. Moreover, a particular strength of the *Detroit Future Youth Curriculum Mixtape* is its incorporation of play as a method of critical inquiry and knowledge production. For example, Young Nation offers the "Hopes + Worries Relay Race" as a fun way to explore obstacles and opportunities emerging from lived experiences of oppression, and the organization offers practitioners ways to move from the "hopes and worries" identified through play to brainstorming programmatic values, guidelines, and courses of action.

While the *Detroit Future Youth Curriculum Mixtape* offers youth and adult allies many opportunities to reflect on and transform the experiences of social inequality that emerge from differences of race and class, there are fewer opportunities to think through experiences of difference that emerge from understandings of sexuality and gender expression. For example, in the *Detroit Future Youth Curriculum Mixtape*, curriculum chapters on the Michigan Roundtable and the Ruth Ellis Center are the only places where sexuality and gender expression are explicitly identified as sites of inquiry and transformation. To build on the explorations of sexual and gender literacy present in these two chapters, community practitioners will need to consult other, perhaps more radical, materials.

Here, *Freeing Ourselves: A Guide to Health and Self Love for Brown Bois* stands as a critical resource for community practitioners interested in weaving a more complex engagement with diverse experiences of sexuality and gender expression into their community literacy projects. A publication of the Brown Boi Project—defined in the text as "a community of masculine of center womyn, men, two-spirit people, transmen, and ... allies ... committed to transforming our privilege of masculinity, gender, and race into tools for achieving Racial and Gender Justice"—*Freeing Ourselves* is a community-based literacy text that broadly addresses health and well-being (4). From their focus on justice—broadly and inclusively defined—the Brown Boi Project frames *Freeing Ourselves* as a community resource for challenging the dominant narratives that reduce gender nonconforming and masculine of center people of color to problems in need of fixing (8).

Chapter One of *Freeing Ourselves*, "Rooted in Spirit: Addressing Mental, Emotional and Spiritual Health," challenges dominant and oppressive understandings of masculinity that discourage and pathologize emotional vulnerability. Grounded in an understanding of European colonization as a process through which indigenous and other ways of understanding and expressing "spiritual, emotional, and psychological health" (14) are marginalized or erased, the chapter focuses on ways to develop the "strong sense of self" (16-17) needed to engage in, and challenge, dominant practices of Western healthcare. To this end, the chapter offers first-person accounts of people's experiences on the path to self-care and a strong sense of self, demonstrating the storytelling practice that the *Detroit Future Youth Curriculum Mixtape* asserts as a powerful tool for transforming injustice and sustaining youth coalition.

Chapter Two, "Free Yourself ... Finding Healthcare Allies," posits that trips to healthcare providers can be an important part of holistic wellness, and acknowledges the often invisible or devalued experiences with healthcare, including inequality with respect to access, that can emerge for gender nonconforming and masculine of center people of color. Chapter Two thus offers full-color tables and illustrations to help people practice a broad and more inclusive understanding of physical wellbeing and develop more effective strategies for practicing a strong sense of self in healthcare contexts.

Chapter Three, "Body Taboo: Getting Down about Sex, Pregnancy, and Menstruation," begins with a frank discussion of sexually transmitted infections and provides full-color tables of terms and definitions as a way of practicing and circulating community-based sexual literacies. The chapter offers this information in a sex-positive light that encourages sexual exploration and pleasure in the context of consenting, communicative encounters. Sexual and gender literacies, in this book, are about both protection and pleasure, and the book acknowledges the body—in addition to resources that emerge from more radical community literacy projects—as an important site of, and tool for, expressing and accessing knowledges of healthy sexuality, broadly and radically defined.

Chapter Four, "Holistic Care through Gender Transition," and Chapter Five, "Energy, Diet, and Physical Practice," offer holistic paths through which gender nonconforming and masculine of center people of color can explore options for maintaining healthy well-being and a strong sense of self during and after gender transition. Across these chapters, the authors encourage readers to take a broader view of health and well-being—one that not only incorporates sexual and gender literacies, but also includes storytelling and resource-sharing as necessary and radical community literacy practices.

In the final, brief chapter, "Brown Boi Manifesto," the authors assert the value of the body in the face of dominant narratives and practices that marginalize gender nonconforming and masculine of center people of color through "one-dimensional representations" (118). Against these flat and flattening representations, the Brown Boi Project asserts the following:

> As individuals and communities existing at the cross-section of multiple oppressions, we first reclaim our true selves from internalized stories of inferiority or gender superiority and celebrate the immeasurable value of all our lives. We will work to take back our decision making power from those who do not hold our best interests at heart. And through these excavations, will carve out in ourselves the capacity for greater choices and love. (118-19)

Here, the Brown Boi Project underscores the harmful ways in which dominant narratives work to discipline and fix bodies, punishing those who defy legibility according to heteronormative alignments of race, gender, sex, and sexuality. Against these restrictive and reductive understandings of identities in motion, the Brown Boi Project asserts the power in locating, recognizing, and circulating—through community literacy projects like *Freeing Ourselves*—the "greater choices" that emerge when truths are told, stories are shared, and community literacies are made known.

The *Detroit Future Youth Curriculum Mixtape* shares these commitments to the transformative potential of storytelling as a community-based literacy practice. Where the *Curriculum Mixtape* leaves room for a more thorough consideration of sexuality and gender expression, *Freeing Ourselves* offers an example of community-based storytelling that reclaims historically devalued knowledges and produces new ones. And where *Freeing Ourselves* leaves room for a more thorough consideration of community-based activism through multimedia and creative expressions via social media, the *Curriculum Mixtape* offers a wealth of examples for engaging youth and adult allies in workshops focused on the multimodal exploration and transformation of dominant stereotypes emerging from reductive and oppressive understandings of difference.

Works Cited

Cole, B., and Luna Han, eds. *Freeing Ourselves: A Guide to Health and Self Love for Brown Bois*. Oakland: Brown Boi Project, 2011. Print.

Detroit Future Youth. *Detroit Future Youth Curriculum Mixtape*. Detroit: Detroit Future Youth, n.d. Print.

Flower, Linda. *Community Literacy and the Rhetoric of Public Engagement*. Carbondale: Southern Illinois UP, 2008. Electronic book.

Madden, Mary, Amanda Lenhart, Maeve Duggan, Sandra Cortesi, and Urs Gasser. *Teens and Technology 2013*. Washington, D.C.: Pew Research Center's Internet & American Life Project, 2013. PDF file.

Sedgwick, Eve Kosofsky. *Epistemology of the Closet*. Berkeley: U of California P, 2008. Print.

Londie T. Martin is a Crossroads Scholar and Assistant Professor in the School of Information Resources & Library Sciences at the University of Arizona. She received her Ph.D. in Rhetoric and Composition Studies from the University of Arizona (londiem@email.arizona.edu).

Respect Yourself, Protect Yourself: Latina Girls and Sexual Identity

Lorena Garcia

NYU Press, 2012. 219 pp.
ISBN 9780814733172. $24.00

Reviewed by Jenna Vinson
University of Massachusetts-Lowell

Sociologist Lorena Garcia's transdisciplinary book, *Respect Yourself, Protect Yourself: Latina Girls and Sexuality*, considers the ways in which Latina youth gain sexual literacy in cultural and community contexts that construct youth sexuality, particularly Latina/o youth sexuality, as risky, crisis-inducing behavior. Through intersectional analysis of interviews with self-identified sexually active Latina young women and their mothers, Garcia moves us beyond pathologizing stereotypes of Latinas and Latina/o culture to a broader understanding of Latina sexuality—one that makes young Latinas legible to readers as youth who are making meaning of their sexual practices and choices as well as their lives.

In this book, Garcia draws attention to the fact that we often want young people to "practice safe sex," but we do not often consider the challenges and constraints that they (particularly young women) must negotiate to do so. In response, Garcia presents findings from participant observations and two years of in-depth interviews with 40 second-generation Mexican and Puerto Rican young women, as well as 18 mothers, living in working-class areas of Chicago. Garcia finds that Latina girls value safe sex as a practice that leads to sexual respectability and a brighter future, but they face many challenges to practicing safe sex, such as family restrictions on time outside of the home and sex education classes that reinforce racial and gender stereotypes rather than teach safe sex practices. Applying an intersectional framework that refuses to generalize about "Latina/o culture," Garcia's analysis engenders insights not only into how young Latinas understand their sexuality, but also into what shapes that understanding: their mother's messages, cultural discourses about race, gender, class, and age, and structural constraints. She approaches mothers and daughters as cultural actors making conflicted choices that, at once, resist certain stereotypes and power relations and, at the same time, support gendered and sexualized hierarchies.

The book is organized into six chapters, each opening with engaging vignettes that reflect Garcia's observations in the community. In chapter one, aptly titled "Studying the 'Other' Girls," Garcia outlines the purpose of the book: to challenge one-dimensional views of young Latinas as always only "at risk" for pregnancy or sexually transmitted diseases, or as part of a "crisis" of unprotected, promiscuous youth. Garcia shifts attention from youth sexuality as a "problem" (which, she argues, also tends to focus on the actions of girls, particularly women of color) toward considerations of how young Latinas understand and practice safe sex and sexual pleasure. Drawing on feminist, race/ethnic, and queer studies, as well as scholarship from sociology and history, Garcia articulates an intersectional theoretical framework that considers "intersecting or interlocking relationships that link social formations such as race/ethnicity, class, gender, sexuality, and age" (8). She then describes her ethnographic method, highlighting her efforts to acknowledge and value her participants' knowledges and needs. One particularly beautiful section of this chapter considers Garcia's insider/outsider role as a community researcher. Drawing on the work of Nancy Naples, Garcia considers how her position as a second-generation young Latina from the Chicago area shaped her interactions with her similarly positioned participants.

Chapters two and three consider the impact of the social institutions often charged with the responsibility of teaching young women about sexual health: family (read: mothers) and school. In chapter two, "'She's Old School Like That': Mother and Daughter Sex Talks," Garcia explores how first-generation Mexican and Puerto Rican mothers respond to the discovery of their daughters' sexual activity, and what daughters think about these responses. Garcia helps readers understand how mothers shape the sexual knowledge and experiences of Latina young women, while being careful not to homogenize Latinidad by consistently drawing attention to differences based on the daughters' sexual orientation and the family's ethnic background. Since racial and gendered scripts construct mothers as "good" or "bad" depending on their daughters' sexual behaviors and outcomes, Garcia argues that there is much at stake for Latina mothers when their daughters are sexually active. Participants' stories demonstrate that Latina mothers actively respond to their daughters' sexuality by communicating to them the importance of "respecting" oneself enough to practice safe sex, by sharing their own experiences to emphasize that sexual activity can make young women more vulnerable to gender and racial inequalities that Latinas already face, and by requesting that family members or female friends also talk to their daughters about sex. This chapter challenges assumptions that Latina mothers are silent on the subject of sexuality by showing how "they engage and rework meanings of gender and sexuality" in responding to their daughters' sexuality.

In chapter three, "The Sexual (Mis)Education of Latina Girls," Garcia presents what young Latina women think of the sex education they received in middle school. Garcia continues to frame Latinas as knowledge- and information-seekers by showing that young Latinas find sex education lacking in providing relevant or useful information to help them negotiate their sexuality. Garcia's participants offer explicit examples of teachers privileging heterosexuality, reinforcing good girl/ bad girl dichotomies, silencing students' questions, and operating from taken-for-granted assumptions of Latinas as destined to become pregnant. Garcia closes this chapter by considering how and why Latina girls in her ethnography seemed to want to do things the "right way"—postponing pregnancy until after they establish a career and household, for instance—in order to challenge stereotypes about Latinas and to benefit their families who did not have similar opportunities in Mexico or Puerto Rico. Encouraged by sex education discourses and broader neoliberal messages, Latina young women seek knowledge about safe sex in order to defy stereotypes and achieve success.

Chapters four and five focus on how Latina young women define and practice safe sex, while also offering some insights into how they discuss (or do not discuss) pleasure. In chapter four, "'Handlin' Your Business': Sexual Respectability and Peers," Garcia shows how many of her participants emphasized the importance of "handlin' your business," or using safe sex practices to "avoid pregnancy and STDs" (84). Garcia observed young women sharing information about sexual health and helping each other access necessary resources. By demonstrating "sexual respectability" through safe sex practices, Latina young women believed they could sustain a social status as good, sexually responsible young women. In other words, participants avoided the "bad girl" label of a sexually active girl by being a sexually responsible girl. Although Garcia finds that her participants resist discourses that would deny them the right to enjoy or engage in sexual activity, she points out that young Latinas still form their sexual subjectivity by distinguishing themselves from "bad" girls they see as irresponsible—like young mothers, or young women who seem promiscuous. This continued good/bad dichotomy made it difficult for heterosexual young women to openly discuss pleasure with friends or partners, although Garcia finds that young lesbian women seemed more comfortable doing so.

In chapter five, Garcia shares participants' stories of negotiating safe sex with partners who often resisted open discussions of sexual safety because they saw them as irrelevant—young heterosexual men believing that, because they are loyal, their partners should trust them, and young lesbian women resisting such conversations because there is less emphasis on lesbian women as "at risk" for negative outcomes. This chapter demonstrates how Latina young women creatively tap into cultural discourses of masculinity and femininity, as well as media depictions of negative outcomes of sex, to initiate productive discussions, and ensure that their partners practice safe sex. However, this chapter again highlights how young heterosexual Latina women feel uncomfortable in openly discussing sexual pleasure with partners.

In the conclusion, Garcia synthesizes her findings and points to practical implications. She writes, "As I listened to the girls' stories about their sex education, I could not help wondering what their sex education experiences would have been like had they had been given an opportunity to share with the adults making sex decisions for them what they felt they needed to learn" (156). Garcia calls us to get over the discomfort we feel about young women having sexual intercourse and, instead, to draw on these young women's experiences and sex-related questions to design accessible and applicable sex education.

While Latina youth are all too often marked by deficit and deficiency, Garcia's book represents young Latinas as intelligent and thoughtful seekers of knowledge and information. This approach makes the book one that could easily accompany other texts working toward asset-driven approaches to non-dominant communities and their particular literacies.

While the book resists many other stereotypes about young Latinas, it does not challenge pathologized representations of young motherhood. A fuller explanation of Garcia's decision not to include pregnant or mothering young Latinas in her inquiry into understandings and practices of sexual safety and pleasure (perhaps reflecting her need to delimit the parameters of the study), could have helped Garcia distinguish the absence of young mothers' perspectives in her book from ongoing efforts to construct young mothers as always and only examples of women who failed to practice safe sex.

The strengths of this book, however, far outweigh any weaknesses. For community literacy researchers and those involved in relevant community/ academic collaborations, this book demonstrates the value of researching all kinds of literacy, even sexual literacy, as ways of knowing, being, and doing that are community-informed and important for improving approaches to education. Garcia's interviews highlight the fact that knowledge about sexuality, gender, race, and inequality is exchanged through literacy practices such as family *testimonios,* health websites, community organizations, peer interactions, media, and partner negotiations.

In addition, since Garcia situates her study as part of work that considers sexuality and gender as socially constructed, and always sites of struggle, this book is especially relevant for Gender, Sexuality, and Women's Studies classrooms. Garcia's intersectional analysis is brilliant as she always considers how patterns in mothers' and daughters' responses and actions reflect larger cultural discourses about women, motherhood, sexuality, race, or class. She is careful not to homogenize Latinas. She also carefully deliberates the complex, and sometimes contradictory, ways in which certain responses resist stereotypes or specifically gendered/raced performances while bolstering instantiations of patriarchy or heteronormativity.

Jenna Vinson is a Crossroads Scholar and Assistant Professor of English at the University of Massachusetts-Lowell (jenna_vinson@uml.edu).

PARLOR PRESS
EQUIPMENT FOR LIVING

New Releases Fall 2013

A Rhetoric for Writing Program Administrators
  Edited by Rita Malenczyk. 471 pages.
Thirty-two contributors delineate the major issues and questions in the field of writing program administration and provide readers new to the field with theoretical lenses through which to view major issues and questions.

Writing Program Administration and the Community College
  Heather Ostman. 241 pages.
From the history of the community college in the United States to current issues and concerns facing writing programs and their administrators and instructors, *Writing Program Administration and the Community College* offers a comprehensive look into writing programs at the public two-year institutions.

Recently Released...

The WPA Outcomes Statement—A Decade Later
  Edited by Nicholas N. Behm, Gregory R. Glau, Deborah H. Holdstein, Duane Roen, and Edward M. White.

Writing Program Administration at Small Liberal Arts Colleges
  Jill M. Gladstein and Dara Rossman Regaignon.

Rewriting Success in Rhetoric and Composition Careers
  Edited by Amy Goodburn, Donna LeCourt, and Carrie Leverenz.

and with the WAC Clearinghouse...

Writing Programs Worldwide: Profiles of Academic Writing in Many Places
  Edited by Chris Thaiss, Gerd Bräuer, Paula Carlino, Lisa Ganobcsik-Williams, and Aparna Sinha

International Advances in Writing Research: Cultures, Places, Measures
  Edited by Charles Bazerman, Chris Dean, Jessica Early, Karen Lunsford, Suzie Null, Paul Rogers, and Amanda Stansell

www.parlorpress.com

www.ingramcontent.com/pod-product-compliance
Lightning Source LLC
Chambersburg PA
CBHW031334160426
43196CB00007B/691